MW00366799

Everyday Book Marketing

Also by Midge Raymond

Everyday Writing: Tips and prompts to fit
your regularly scheduled life

Forgetting English: Stories

For Kate —

Everyday Book Marketing

*Promotion ideas to fit your
regularly scheduled life*

With very best wishes
for a successful book
launch & beyond!

Midge Raymond

**Ashland
Creek
Press**

Everyday Book Marketing

Promotion ideas to fit your regularly scheduled life

Published by Ashland Creek Press

www.ashlandcreekpress.com

© 2013 Midge Raymond

All rights reserved. No part of this book may be reproduced or transmitted, in any form or by any means, without written permission of the publisher.

ISBN 978-1-61822-027-1

Library of Congress Control Number: 2013934805

Printed in the United States of America on acid-free paper.

All paper products used to create this book are Sustainable Forestry Initiative (SFI) Certified Sourcing.

Contents

Intro

When my first book was published, I knew I had a lot of work to do. For one, the book was a short story collection, a genre that is not exactly wildly popular with mainstream readers. In addition, the collection was published by a university press, which by definition means a small staff and small budget. Not only that—unbeknownst to its authors, the press was about to close its doors, and before my book was released, half the staff had been laid off, with the few remaining staff members juggling the work of the entire press.

Needless to say, when it came to promotion, I was on my own.

While it was pretty disheartening at the time, I've come to realize that I wasn't at all alone—and that this learning process was time very well spent. The vast majority of authors, whether self-published or traditionally published, are largely in charge of their own marketing, and the trial-by-fire I went through gave me the tools I needed as an author. Granted, a great many readers have still never heard of me—but my book did go into a second printing before its original publisher closed, is now enjoying a new life in a second edition from another independent press, and has a robust digital life as well, selling in countries from North America to Europe to Australia.

But none of this happens on its own.

Today's author plays not only the role of Writer but also of Publicist and Director of Sales & Marketing. Depending on the type of publishing agreement, an author today may be in charge of anything from writing his own cover copy to sending out her own review copies. In addition, the entire publishing industry is in a state of flux and likely will be for quite some time. As I often tell my fellow writers, all of this can be so challenging and so time-consuming that it actually makes writing look like the easy part (and that's really saying something).

Who this book is for...

I wrote this book for several reasons. For one, I wanted to share all that I've learned over the years—not only as a writer but as someone who's worked in publishing for two decades, from working for traditional New York publishers in the 1990s to becoming a co-founder of a boutique press in 2011. Publishing has changed tremendously during the last couple of decades, and more changes are sure to come (among them: at the time of this writing, the Big Six publishers are on the verge of becoming the Big Five, due to the merger of Penguin and Random House). Having become a published writer amid all these changes in the industry and in technology has been enlightening and invigorating, and future authors are sure to find similar opportunities and challenges.

Second, I wanted to share what I've learned about book marketing on a strict budget, not only of money but of time. Some authors have publishers who pay for advertising, review copies, and book tours; many of us aren't as fortunate. Some authors have the luxury of time, money, and freedom to travel to events, book festivals, and conferences; others have to consider jobs, child care, and finances first.

I wrote this book with the Everyday Writer in mind—the

published author who is not only a writer but also has a career, a family, and/or any number of other obligations that require fitting book promotion into a budget in which both hours and dollars may be hard to find.

This book is for all writers who have published a book or are on their way to publication, by whatever means, whether it's traditional publishing or self-publishing. This book aims to teach you cost-effective ways to promote your book, from scheduling a book tour to making the most of social media.

Most important is to keep in mind that while the months leading up to your book launch date are vital, promotion is by no means finished a few months after publication. Promotion is, in many ways, a journey without an end. But, well managed, it can be a fulfilling journey.

How to use this book...

Readers who are still many months away from publication will get the most of out of this book, but even if your book has already been released, you'll learn tips for how to keep the buzz going, how to continue to find new readers, and how to build upon what you learn as you go through this process, which will be unique to each writer. I recommend reading the whole book through even if you're not at a certain stage in the process yet—for example, you'll want to learn why, in the **Book Launch and Beyond** section, it's important to prepare for readings even before your book goes into print.

The first section, **Think Outside the Book**, is designed to help you begin the transition from Writer to Marketing Expert.

The second section, **First Things First: Book Marketing Basics**, covers the things you'll need to take care of before publication (that is, once you have a book contract with a publisher or once you decide to self-publish). This includes everything from building a website to planning events to getting familiar with social media.

The third section, **Book Launch and Beyond**, offers tips and advice for not only how to have a successful book launch but also how to keep the buzz going on an everyday basis.

This section will include advice for how to stay involved in the process of promoting your book, whether you have ten minutes a day or two hours.

The fourth and last section features **Q&As with Authors and Experts**, featuring a range of writers and industry experts—from librarians to fiction authors to poets—who provide invaluable tips on everything from how to present yourself as an author to how to reach out to event venues. You'll hear from authors who've published with big houses and with small presses, as well as from self-published authors. You'll hear from authors who have published one book and those who have published dozens. You'll also hear from experts with wide-ranging experiences in the book industry, offering such tips as how to approach bookstores and book reviewers, how to find the right photographer for your author photo, and how to effectively promote your events from the ground up. These are people who, quite simply, love what they do, in whatever way it involves books, and I'm delighted that they are willing to share their experiences with me so that I can share them with you.

And, finally, throughout the pages of this book, you'll encounter **Everyday Marketing Tips** designed to help you complete the most essential marketing tasks even when you're short on time.

Part 1:
Think Outside the Book

Transitioning from Writer to Marketing Expert

As anyone who has published a book knows, the promotion can be just as much work as the writing itself—if not more. And promotion can be particularly challenging for writers who are far more comfortable in the solitude of their writing spaces than in front of audiences, as well as for those time-strapped authors who managed to find time to finish their books in the early or late hours of the day but now may have to find time during more normal hours to promote it.

Thanks to the Internet, it's possible to promote your book without leaving your home. It's not ideal—most readers love the opportunity to meet writers—but even if you're only able to schedule a few in-person events, you can do a lot on social networks and on a "virtual" book tour.

It's also possible, if you start at least six months before your book's release date, to accomplish all you need to do within an hour or so a day—it's a question of knowing what you need to do, getting organized, and making the most of the moments you have.

First, you'll need to transition from writer to marketer. This is often a difficult transition for a writer who only wants to start on her next project—but while it's great (and essential) to keep up with your writing, you don't want to do this entirely at the expense of the book you've just worked so hard to finish and get out into the world. And with more than 200,000 books being published each year and so much competition for every reader's attention, you need to be willing to get out there (in person and/or virtually) to talk about your book. If you're not out there talking about your book, you're likely to find that no one else is talking about it either.

The next section will give you an idea of the specifics you need to think about, but in the meantime, here are a few big-picture questions to consider as you make this transition into marketing mode.

How is your book coming into the world?

Whether you're being published by a large publisher, by a small press, or self-publishing will determine much of your marketing plan. If you have a large house behind you, you may have access to a great deal of its resources (on the other hand, as Kim Wright points out in her Q&A on page 132, you may not). If you publish with a small press, you may be able to work closely with your publisher to share marketing opportunities. If you self-publish, you'll have to be especially creative—and also have partners willing to help (see Zoe Ghahremani's Q&A on page 173 for more about this). If you publish an e-book only, you'll be doing online marketing since you don't have a physical product (or you may decide, as Jackie Bouchard discusses in her Q&A on page 188, that having a print copy is worthwhile for the marketing opportunities it offers). But do keep in mind that, in whatever way your book is entering the world, you'll need to prepare yourself for a lot of promotion ahead.

Who's the audience for your book?

If you publish traditionally, your book will be categorized by your publisher; talk to your editor and/or publicist about how they plan to market it—as literary fiction, or women's fiction? as general fiction, or mystery? Not that you have to follow their category for your book, but how it's labeled by your publisher allows you to tap into certain markets. For example, if your publisher is labeling your novel as a romance, this opens up a lot of opportunities with book bloggers, romance writers' associations, etc.

Another thing to consider is the way readers are most likely to discover your book. If you self-publish, you may find that your core audience is primarily digital, as bestselling Kindle author L.J. Sellers has learned (see her Q&A on page 159). If you're publishing on your own, providing lower-priced e-books is a great way to get your work into the hands of new readers who are more likely to take a chance on a new author if it doesn't cost them very much. And then, if these readers like your book, word of mouth (via good online reviews) will keep the buzz going.

What are the best ways to reach your intended audience?

You'll want to go where your readers are. If they're mystery fans, check out the big mystery conferences, such as Bouchercon, Malice Domestic, and Left Coast Crime. If it's literary fiction, look into such conferences as AWP (Association of Writers & Writing Programs) and Bread Loaf. You'll also want to explore the myriad venues where you can plan book-related events; see Part 2 for more on events.

What resources will you need to promote your book?

This includes everything from money to time. Part 2 covers book marketing basics, such as a website and author photo—but even before you get to this, consider what your budget is and how much money you can afford to devote to promoting your book. This will help you plan, and stick to, a reasonable budget (see Wendy Call's Q&A on page 144 for tips and advice on creating a budget).

Next, think about what sort of time you have to spend on promotion. Ideally, you'll be able to devote at least three-quarters of your writing time (if not all of it, for the next six to twelve months) on book promotion instead. Book promotion can be endless—you'll realize that there's always more you can be doing—so you'll need to be sure you do the minimum while still keeping your regularly scheduled life in some sort of order. Figure out ways to maximize your book promotion time for the next six to twelve months, whether it means getting up earlier, finding child care, recruiting family members to take on some of your usual duties, etc. Remember, your book's launch happens only once, so you'll want to make it count.

A word about independent publicists: Depending on how you publish, you may or may not have an in-house publicist who will work with you on your book promotion—and even if you do, this publicist will likely have several, or many, other authors to promote as well. So, if your budget allows, you might consider hiring an independent publicist to work with you (this person can also work with your in-house publicist). See the Q&A with publicist Alice B. Acheson on page 196 for more details on how an independent publicist can help.

What will work best with your strengths and schedule?

This is where you'll need to be most honest and realistic with yourself. Many writers, for example, feel they must do readings as part of a book tour—yet this is only one of many options for a book tour. And if you're the parent of a small child, perhaps doing a multi-city tour isn't going to work; focus instead on making the most of local events, and do other events virtually. If you're a serious introvert, maybe in-person events will cause more stress than they're worth, or won't allow you to fully connect with readers; focus more on writing guest blogs, op-eds, essays, and articles, and submit them widely. Or, on the other hand, if blogging and social media don't come naturally to you, focus instead on opportunities that you do enjoy. While book promotion does require that we leave our normal comfort zones—by reading in public, for example, or by writing and submitting op-eds—it needn't be (and shouldn't be) torture. Know that you'll need to do some things that will be challenging; also be prepared to recognize your own strengths and weaknesses and arrange your book marketing around ways that capitalize on your strengths while minimizing the activities that are more difficult.

Part 2:
First Things First: Book Marketing Basics

This section covers what you'll need to know—and accomplish—well before your book is released. If your book launch is scheduled for next week, not to worry; you've probably done many of these things already, and late is always better than never. And if you've got six months or more before your book's publication, fantastic—laying the groundwork is especially important before your book is published, so that you're ready to go and not catching up. By taking care of these pre-publication items well before your book launch, you'll find that you'll be well equipped to handle the flurry of activity that surrounds you around the launch date.

Before Publication

ALIGN YOUR PUBLISHING METHOD WITH YOUR GOALS

As you'll see in the Q&As in the last section of this book, there are myriad opportunities for you as an author no matter how you ultimately choose to publish. However, it's good to make sure that you're realistic about your goals before embarking on the journey of book promotion. If you've self-published, for example, you will need to be prepared to offer your book to bookstores on consignment, and to know that local bookstores are likely to be your best bet (though this doesn't mean you shouldn't try other bookstores!). If your book is available only in digital format, it obviously makes more sense to do a virtual tour than an in-person tour. If you've published with a small press, you need to make sure your book will be sent out for reviews and/or awards—and if not, budget for this yourself. And if you're with a large publisher but you're not one of its bigger authors, work with the company to fill in any gaps there might be along the way.

And also keep in mind that nothing in this industry is

definite or absolute—all writers have unique relationships with their communities and with their readers. So while some marketing tactics may work better for you depending on how you publish, every section of this book is designed to help the writer who has a book to share, no matter how it ultimately arrives in the world.

TAKE AN AUTHOR PHOTO

I can still remember the days (long ago) when an author's photo on a book cover was optional. Sometimes you'd see one, often in black-and-white, and sometimes not. Now, however, in these days of "mediagenic" authors and digital imagery, the author photo is no longer an option. Which is a little stressful for those of us who have a disproportionate number of bad hair days or who may not love the camera.

Yet we all have to do it—these days, authors are expected to have a photo not only on a book cover but also on a website and in any publicity material surrounding the book. And given the range of options out there, your author photo can work either for or against you. A great author photo can be inviting and can encourage readers to want to read your book; on the other hand, a poorly taken photo or strangely staged shot can turn off readers. Here are a few tips for making your author photo experience as stress-free as possible, and for making the photo itself as accessible as it can be.

Determine your budget, and stay within it.
Otherwise, you're sure to be even more stressed about your author photo. There's nothing worse than spending money you don't have—unless it's on a photo that will remind you

of it at every turn. Many wonderful photographers out there know that we writers don't make a lot of money; find one that you can afford, then relax and enjoy the process.

Invest in a good camera.

If you can't afford a photographer—or if a set of author shots costs more than a decent camera—invest in a camera yourself, and learn to use it well (or find someone who already knows). Not only will you be able to use the camera for your Official Author Photo, but the investment will pay off in many other ways. For one, you can take photos on your book tour and at other events, which are always nice to have. Two, you can take a few good shots to offer in addition to your Official Author Photo, just for a little variety. And keep in mind that taking your own, less formal shot might be a great way to go, especially if you've got a tight budget or if you don't like the more formal studio shots. The photo on the cover of this book was taken by my husband (who put himself through college in part by working as a photographer), and while it's not a professional studio shot, I like the more casual feel of it.

Be yourself.

Have you ever been to a reading where you couldn't identify the author because he/she looked so unlike the photo on the book cover? Beware of this. You'll want to look your best, but don't go too crazy with hair, makeup, or clothing; most of all, you'll want to look like yourself. And, while it's certainly tempting, avoid using a photo that captures your youthful self but doesn't at all resemble your current self. And, if possible, replace your author photo every five years, give or take, especially if you've published additional books; again, you'll want to be recognizable, as well as up-to-date.

Don't get too creative.

We've all seen author photos in which the author looks uncomfortable, angry, or even downright scary in trying to achieve a certain look. While a simple head shot can seem boring, it's usually better than a bizarre pose or something too staged. Try to go for a casual, friendly, accessible look. And also consider the subject matter of your book. If your novel is about the Holocaust or 9/11, perhaps a beaming author photo isn't the way to go; on the other hand, if you've written a comedy, looking too serious might lead readers to believe you're not all that witty.

Interview photographers.

This is a great idea no matter what, but especially if you're going to spend a lot of money. Once you've narrowed down your list based on the portfolios you like the best, schedule a meeting or a chat. Make sure the photographer knows exactly what you want and can achieve this for you. And make sure it's someone you feel comfortable with, or you won't be looking very relaxed in your photos. See the Q&A on page 204 with photographer Rosanne Olson, who regularly takes photos for writers and other artists, for what to look for in a photographer.

Everyday Marketing Tips

Fifteen-minute marketing: Set aside fifteen minutes a day to research photographers in your area and price range. (If you're getting close to book launch time, up this to thirty minutes until you find the right fit.) Note: Consider friends, family members, neighbors, etc., especially if your budget doesn't allow for a professional shot—you may find photographic talent lurking where you least expect it.

Everyday marketing: As you go about your usual routine getting dressed and ready for the day ahead, think about what clothing, hairstyle, etc., you'd like to sport for your author photo. Thinking about this daily will give you a good idea of what you like and don't like, and can save you a lot of time and stress on the day of the photo shoot.

CREATE AN AUTHOR BIO

This is extremely obvious, but I'm including this here because so many authors find the idea of writing their own mini-biography so intimidating—and it certainly can be. There are myriad ways to do it, for one; and two, how do you decide what to include and what to leave out?

First, spend some time going through books and websites and reading author bios. You may need to read ten, or you may need to read a hundred—but read until you get a good idea of what you enjoy learning about an author. Be sure to check out the bios of your favorite authors as well as those you're unfamiliar with. You'll notice that some bios are very factual; they include a few words about publication history and nothing else. Others include information about an author's family, non-writing work, hometown, and pets. On many author websites, you'll find bios that are written by authors in the first person, detailing everything from when they were born up until the time their books were published.

After exploring other authors' bios, you'll get a feel for what you'd like to do for your own. While there are no rules, I recommend creating two bios—one that is a few sentences long, and another that is a few paragraphs long. This way, you'll be able to furnish a longer, more detailed bio if anyone ever needs it (a newspaper reporter, for example, or a book reviewer), and you'll also have a short one ready for those who want only a few words—and both are important to have available so you don't have to scramble to pull something together.

Personally, I am in the less-is-more camp—my standard bio is a few sentences long and includes my books, awards, a few journals I've published in, and the general region in which I work and live. Other times, it's shorter than that—if I'm asked for something longer, I'll include a bit more work experience, write about what inspires my writing, and mention that I live with my husband and an opinionated orange cat. That's about as personal as I get in a written bio—but that's just me. Other writers are more comfortable revealing information about their childhoods, their families, and other things that inform their writing lives—and this is wonderful, as many readers like learning all there is to know about authors. Just be sure you're comfortable with what you're putting out there in writing for all the world to see—sometimes more privacy is better.

Most of all, try to find a balance between offering a sense of yourself as a person and as an author (and this may include work rather than personal details), while maintaining a little privacy as well. After all, one nice thing about going on a book tour is to offer readers something they can't get from your bio—so sometimes a little bit less can be a little bit more in the end.

CREATE A WEBSITE

A website is essential for authors, though it needn't be expensive or high-end. You simply need to have an online presence so that readers, potential reviewers or interviewers, or anyone else interested in your book can find and contact you. And of course, it's a great place to highlight your book and other related work.

One question I hear often from not-yet-published writers is: "Do I need a website if I don't have a book?" And there are a couple of answers to this question, depending on the writer and his/her goals. For one, if you have a book in the works with every intention of publishing it (i.e., you have a contract or plan to self-publish), you should go ahead and start planning a website. And "planning" can mean anything from surfing around to see what author sites you like best to interviewing web designers. But if you don't have a completed book just yet, your time may be better spent finishing the book than creating a website. For now, anyway. (Trust me, writing the next book is even harder when you have a website to procrastinate with.) There's really no downside to having an author website at any time—especially if you're widely published in a lot of journals, or if you do a lot of teaching—but if you don't have a book to sell or events to list, there's no huge hurry to get it up there, either.

A good author website should include:

- a home page with the latest news
- a page/section listing your upcoming and past events
- a book page with your book's cover image and description, as well as a link to an excerpt from your book (a PDF of the first chapter, for example)

- a bio page with your photo and a brief biography with details relevant to your work

- reviews and blurbs

- a reading guide and/or discussion questions (for classrooms and/or book clubs)

- a book club contact form or e-mail address

- a blog (see page 35)

- links to where readers can buy your book

- links to your Facebook, Twitter, and/or other social media pages

- a contact form or e-mail address for contacting you

- a way for readers to "subscribe" to hear about your news and events (see page 44)

So, how to go about creating a website? Below are a few things to consider before you begin, followed by details on author website essentials.

First, spend some time on author websites to discover what you like. You'll want your own site to emulate what you like about your favorite author sites, whether it's the bio page or the navigation bar. Doing a redesign can be time-consuming and expensive, so you'll want your website to be something you really like from the beginning.

Second, figure out how much time and money you've got to work with. A website needn't be flashy (in fact, the too-flashy sites, with bright colors or lots of animation, can actually irritate visitors)—it only needs to be pleasing to the eye and easy to navigate. Also, think about your domain name; be sure to register both your own name and the title of your book (but host only one—for example, ForgettingEnglish. com redirects to MidgeRaymond.com; this way, I have only one site, but people who remember the book title but not my name will still be able to find me). You can register domains at GoDaddy.com, Register.com, and other sites; many authors also use blog software (such as WordPress) to host their websites, which is very affordable.

Third, define your goals as a writer and how your website will serve these goals. If you're on your sixth book and are ready to step into high gear to brand yourself as a writer, you'll have a lot of content to manage and you might want outside advice and a professional designer. If you're about to publish your first book, you may want a simpler site that focuses on your book and your bio.

And, finally, during the process of creating your website, ask friends and family, fellow writers, and others for their feedback—it can be hard to take a step back and see your site objectively when you've been immersed in the process. Ask them whether they've found everything they need, whether anything was confusing or hard to find, and what might be missing. Consider updating your site every few years— particularly if you have a new book to promote. You don't want to redesign your website so often that you lose your connection with readers, but a nice remodel keeps your site looking and feeling up-to-date. And keep in mind that it doesn't need to be a complete overhaul; even an occasional touch-up helps, such as a new author photo or adding another tab when you publish a new book.

See the next page for a little more detail on the website essentials.

The home page...

This should be welcoming, of course, and also should appear up-to-date. Because I don't always have breaking news for visitors, I simply change the date on my website so that visitors know I'm still alive, still writing, and still doing events and classes from time to time.

The events page...

It goes without saying that you'll want to list your upcoming events. However, it's also good to list your past events as well—this helps with search results, and also gives prospective hosts a good idea of what you've done before. Most important is that you *list your events from most recent to earlier.* Past events should appear at the bottom of the list, upcoming events at the top—otherwise, visitors taking a quick glance your events listing will see only the past events, which will not only look outdated but means they won't see what's next (many readers won't take the time to scroll down to find upcoming events, especially if you have a long list of past events).

The book and/or publications page...

Because *Forgetting English* was my only book for a long time, and because it contains only ten of the dozens of stories I've published, I started out with a tab that read PUBLICATIONS. This allowed me to include *Forgetting English* as well as other short stories that have been published in literary magazines, and it made me feel very prolific. Now I've got a BOOKS tab on my navigation bar, as well as a PUBLICATIONS tab. Publications in magazines and journals appear on the publications page, and the two editions of *Forgetting English*, as well as *Everyday Writing* and *Everyday Book Marketing*, appear on the books page. On your books/publications page, always be sure to include your book's cover image and description, as well as links for where readers can buy it.

Somewhere on your website you'll want to include an excerpt from your book, and the books/publications page is a great place for this link. Posting an excerpt is essential not only for letting readers sample a few pages and fall in love with your book, but it's also helpful for book bloggers who may decide whether to review your book based on a few pages. I've heard from several readers and reviewers that the *Forgetting English* excerpt on my site was what made them take a chance on reading a story collection, sometimes for the first time.

The bio page ...

Go with whatever style biography you prefer (see **Create an author bio**, above), keeping in mind that your website's bio shouldn't be so short that it doesn't offer enough relevant information, or so long that no one will read it. And always include a good, professional photo (see **Take an author photo**, above).

The reviews page ...

Show off your reviews and blurbs wherever you can (this is not the time to be modest), preferably on a dedicated page; you might label it REVIEWS or PRAISE, depending on your initial ratio of reviews to blurbs, but make sure it's easy to find. You can list reviews by date, or even by prominence (i.e., putting a *Publishers Weekly* or *New York Times* review ahead of a blog review). If you have enough awards to warrant an awards page, by all means go for it—otherwise, be sure your awards are listed on your bio page and/or on the book page.

The reading guide or discussion questions...

Whatever the genre of your book, it's a great idea to include a reading guide and/or discussion questions—for use in book clubs, schools, university classrooms, or any other group that may be interested in your book. (My *Forgetting English* reading guide is actually on my blog, but I link to it on my book page so that readers can find it easily.) Include your availability as well as information on how to contact you for speaking events, teaching gigs, or book club meetings (more on book clubs on page 91).

The blog...

Most writers have blogs (more on this on page 35), and I highly recommend that you do as well; it's a great way to keep readers updated on everything from the latest news to upcoming events to new reviews and awards. Your blog could be part of your website or hosted elsewhere—just be sure to include an easy-to-find link.

The links to where readers can find your book...

This is a bit obvious, but I'm always amazed by how often this info gets buried or left off author websites altogether. These links should appear on your home page, or, if you have many books, in prominent spots on your individual book pages. Most authors list any and all possible ways a reader can buy their books, which I'd recommend, as every reader has his or her own preferences, from Amazon to IndieBound. And don't neglect to include links to the indie bookstores that have supported you, as well as to offer signed copies that come directly from you.

The links to social media...

Always include links to Facebook, Twitter, Tumblr, and any other social media on which you're active; this makes it easy for readers to find you and share you. Use those perky little icon buttons, which make them easy to spot, and put them in the upper right corner of every page of your website, where visitors can't miss them.

The way to contact you...

One of the main purposes of a website is to connect with readers—as well as to be accessible to reviewers, reporters, etc. If you are worried about being inundated with spam, use a contact form instead of posting your e-mail address. And always do your best to respond to every (legitimate) e-mail you receive.

The subscribers...

If you haven't already, begin collecting an e-mail list of readers and anyone else interested in your book—this way, you can send Evites or e-mail newsletters to announce your events (see page 44 for more on e-mail marketing). Your website should have at least one link to where people can subscribe to your mailing list, but you'll probably find that there are opportunities to put it in more than one place (mine is in the footer of my website, as well as on my NEWS & EVENTS page).

Everyday Marketing Tips

Fifteen-minute marketing: Take the categories on the previous pages and write them down somewhere convenient, whether a saved file on your desktop or a notebook you carry with you. Whenever you have a few spare moments, tackle one (or more) items on the list, i.e., write up your author bio, choose which excerpt from your book you'll use on your site, jot down a few blog post ideas. Tackling your website all at once can seem overwhelming, but if you gather the pieces together bit by bit, they'll be ready to go when the time comes.

Everyday marketing: Anytime you have a few moments to spare, check out author websites to see what you like—and make a note of why. You may like one author's ABOUT page and another's PUBLICATIONS page; keep notes so that you can custom-design your own website just the way you'd like.

CREATE VISUALS AND GIVEAWAYS

As soon as you have cover art for your book, I recommend creating bookmarks, postcards, and/or business cards with the cover art, a little info about the book, and a little info about you. Depending on what you create, you'll be able to include a lot or a little information.

A **postcard**, for example, can have the cover image on one side and a description of the book, a brief author bio, and publication information on the other; it can also have all the info on one side and room for a mailing address on the other side, though I find that so few people use snail mail anymore that it's probably better to use postcards in other ways. I had postcards made for the first edition of *Forgetting English* but didn't mail them; instead, I put as much info as I could on the cards and handed them out to friends, family, booksellers, librarians, and strangers, and I sent small quantities to folks who offered to do the same. I also pinned them on community bulletin boards, everywhere from the local pub to the mailroom of my apartment building. I also used stickers on the front to announce events, which was a great way to update the postcards constantly without having to print more.

Bookmarks are useful, too; while you can't fit nearly as much information on them, readers tend to hold onto them and share them, and many bookstores and libraries like to have freebies to offer their customers. For the second edition of *Forgetting English*, I printed up bookmarks, and they consistently disappear at events (even if my books don't). The nice thing about a bookmark is that the title, author name, and cover image are out there (also be sure to include the URL for your website), and it will remind readers of your book.

Best of all, if they grab a handful of bookmarks and share them, you may find new readers as well.

Business cards are especially helpful if you do a lot of events and workshops and want to offer such information as your e-mail address and phone number. If possible, choose a card that allows you to have book art on one side; some business cards are designed to fold out and look almost like mini-books. There are myriad designs and formats to choose from once you start looking at vendors.

Speaking of vendors, rest assured that purchasing such items as bookmarks or postcards won't break the bank. Here are a few vendors I've used before that I would recommend for good quality, prices, and service. Please keep in mind that vendors and prices do change, so be sure to investigate on your own—ask for samples, and always be on the lookout for hidden costs and/or fees. Also note that these prices do not include shipping.

Got Print (www.gotprint.net)

Postcards—Standard 4x6 postcards with a matte finish are $70 for 1,000.

Bookmarks—2x7 bookmarks with matte finish are $35 for 500.

For another good option, check out Print Place (www.printplace.com).

BuildaSign.com (www.buildasign.com)

Bumper stickers are $75 for 100.

Sticker Mule (www.stickermule.com)

> The cost for 300 custom stickers ranges from $75 to $175; bumper stickers, sticker sheets, and die-cut stickers cost a bit more.

Busy Beaver Button Company (www.busybeaver.net)

> Custom one-inch buttons with metal pins are $40 for 100.

Moo (www.moo.com)

> Moo is great for high-quality business cards, mini-cards, postcards, greeting cards, and more. Moo is more expensive, but both quality and services are excellent.

Everyday Marketing Tips

Thirty-minute marketing: When you have half an hour to spare, get online and research vendors—as many as you can. Ask other writers you know for recommendations. You may want to take into account not only the cost but your own design skills; for example, if you don't have a lot of design experience, you may find that one vendor is more user-friendly than another and that this is a bigger plus than saving a few dollars.

Everyday marketing: As you go about your regularly scheduled life, take note of the visuals and products that are all around you—flyers at cafés and on bulletin boards, the brochures and rack cards at local businesses—and pay attention to which ones appeal to you, and why. If a fellow writer has a stunning bookmark or business card, ask about the design and printing. Collect the samples you like and keep them in a file so that when you're ready to design your own materials, you'll already have an idea of what you want in terms of color, font, size, etc.

START A BLOG

The first bit of advice most writers get about book promotion is usually "write a blog." And it's great advice. Yet writers often think, "Wait ... I've just spent six years on this novel, and now I have to write more?"

Well, yes.

Of course, some writers end up getting published *because* of their blogs, and if you're writing nonfiction, you're at an advantage; whether it's cooking or travel or advice for moms, nonfiction lends itself well to blogging. And if you're enough of an expert in something to write a book about it, you probably already have a blog, which means you've got a platform and an audience.

But if you're a fiction writer or poet, you may not have considered writing a blog. You may be far more interested in writing drafts of stories and poems than in trying to create content for blog posts and worrying about building an audience. I feel your pain; I put off blogging as long as I could, until I finally caved in 2006. And it has turned out to be a lot more fun than I thought.

When I began my blog, I was juggling a zillion things and barely had time to write as it was—and naturally I wondered why I should write a blog when I could be writing stories. I didn't even have a book to promote at the time. But I'm glad I did begin blogging. The same way teaching helps me practice what I preach in terms of good writing, blogging is helpful in so many ways, from staying on top of publishing news to getting me thinking about new writing rituals to connecting with other readers and writers. And, in addition to enhancing my own work, it's fun. Best of all for the writer with a new or forthcoming book, a blog will allow you to post updates on anything from your area of expertise to the book publication process to your upcoming events.

A good author blog should:

- include news and information that will draw in prospective readers
  - use clear, newsy headlines that can be easily searched
  - use keywords and tags
  - stay focused; feel free to keep posts short
  - use different styles for your posts—a photo one day, a Q&A the next, etc.
  - provide value by linking to other blogs, news articles, etc.
- feature your author photo, bio, book cover image, and links to where to buy the book
- incorporate blurbs, reviews, articles, and other items to help create buzz about your book
- be updated at least once a week, even if briefly, to appear up-to-date
- be open to comments and feedback, to allow for connections with readers
- link to other blogs and foster community
- be attractive and inviting visually

Keep in mind that every author and every book is different, so you should choose blog software—and a blogging style—that fits your needs. Perhaps you're more visual, or you've written a cookbook that depends heavily on photos; if so, Tumblr might be your best choice. Perhaps you're at your best in front of the camera; work YouTube videos into your blog. If you're better at short, pithy bursts of language than longer forms, you may choose to be more active on Twitter than on your blog. It's important to have a strong online presence, but equally important is to honor your strengths and to find your niche.

Keeping in mind that your blog will take one of many forms, here are a few things to keep in mind to help you capture the essentials of a good author blog.

Start now.

As in, right this second. Even if your book isn't due out for another year (or even if you haven't written it yet) you'll want to get started on your blog right away. You need to build content, attract readers, and develop its voice and style. Starting early allows you to take your time and to learn good blogging practices before the pressure's on.

Write what you know.

Nothing fits this adage better than blogging. This is why people blog, after all—to offer their expertise to others. And it's the same reason people read blogs—to learn about things they want or need to know, whether it's how to write dialogue or how to bake a vegan birthday cake. Again, if you're writing nonfiction, you likely have a lot of knowledge to share—but even if you're writing fiction, you can keep a blog about news related to your book, for example, or about your writing life and process, both of which will give readers insight into you and your work.

Post as often as you can...

...without making it too much of a chore. Posting frequently is great, but even more important is that the content is good and useful (see the next tip, below). If you treat blogging as a chore, your readers will probably notice that your heart's not in it. Blogging can be a lot of work, as any blogger will tell you, but you don't have to post that often to have a successful blog—as long as your blog is interesting and relevant, you'll draw in readers. That said, you'll want to blog often enough that readers know your blog is active. Try to post up to three times a week, particularly around book launch time or when you have events coming up—but even if you can only post once or twice a month, that's something. Keep in mind that short posts are okay—and probably much more likely to be read than longer ones.

Be interesting and relevant.

You'll want your blog to have a solid focus but one that also allows for some breathing room. As an example, on my blog, I post a weekly writing exercise, just to be sure I post something at least once a week. Then, if I can, I'll post something else—such as a writing tip, an addition to my "Bookstore Geek" series on fabulous indie bookstores, random thoughts about writing and publishing, or Q&As with other bookish folks. So while it's all writing related, the content itself varies quite a bit.

Have daily/weekly themes, or ongoing topics.

Finding a theme that makes weekly posting easy and fun will help keep you posting—and it'll also give your readers something to keep returning for. My Weekly Writing column, with a new writing exercise every Monday as a jump-start to the week, has been a lot of fun and keeps me posting regularly.

Poet Kelli Russell Agodon (see her Q&A on page 179) features Confession Tuesday on her blog, in which she confesses her "sins," none of which are sinful but all of which we can relate to as humans and as writers.

Be yourself.

Let your voice come through on your blog. You may not want to be quite as colloquial or as open as you are when chatting with your best friends (depending on what you talk about), but don't be shy about showing your personality. That said, keep in mind that everyone from your editor to your employer to your in-laws may be reading your blog at any given time— so be yourself, but with enough restraint to keep you out of trouble.

Be generous.

By highlighting others, you not only have new material to write about, but you're paying it forward. Link to other relevant blogs often; share the love. Offer to do a guest post for another writer's blog, or invite a writer to be a guest on yours. Do a Q&A with a writer you admire, or write up a mini-review of a friend's new book. Sharing is a great way to discover new blogs and to help others discover them as well, and it always returns its rewards.

Be good-looking.

Make sure your blog is neat and organized, ensure that your background colors and images are easy on the eyes, and use a normal-sized, serif font. Use images and video when you can, and keep paragraphs short. Bullets and lists are handy and make for easy reading—remember, no one wants to get bogged down in long paragraphs of text on a computer screen.

A quick note on images: Don't go too crazy (use them only if they're relevant, and avoid generic-looking stock photos), and make sure you have taken the photos yourself or have permission to use them. It may not seem like a big deal to snag a photo from somewhere else, but I know of writers who have done this and have had to pay damages (and this is not cheap) for using photos without permission.

Invite comments—and reply to them.

For the first year of my blog, I didn't open it to comments; I was worried that I'd get a lot of spam, that freaky people would make creepy comments, or that I would get so few comments that my blog would look really sad and pathetic. But after hearing nonstop from media gurus everywhere that there's no point to blogging without welcoming comments, I gave in. And yes, all of the above did happen and still does. But I've found that it's worth it—inviting feedback and creating dialogue has fostered connections and helped build an audience.

Use keywords.

Think of keywords (i.e., words that are relevant to the content of each post) and include them as tags to help draw traffic to your blog—of course, only if they're relevant (if you lure readers to your site with false promises, they won't come back). And keep headlines as simple and user-friendly as possible.

Let people know you're there.

Let everyone in your circles know that you have a blog and invite them to visit and comment. Share posts on social media as well. I usually tweet each new blog post I write, offering a newsy kernel so people will click through if they're interested.

I sometimes mention posts on Facebook as well, or post links on LinkedIn if they might be relevant to my connections there. By the way, while it's possible to network all of your social media together, I don't recommend this (see the sections on social networks, beginning on page 51, for more).

Share the love.
All bloggers like to receive comments; we like to know people are reading our blogs, and comments provide a great indicator. So reach out and comment on blogs that you like; this is good karma, and it's fun. Also, keep a blogroll, linking to other bloggers you follow, who in turn will probably be glad to list you on theirs as well (but don't link to blogs solely with this hope, and don't solicit links from strangers; be genuine).

Everyday Marketing Tips

Thirty-minute marketing: Take half an hour to do a freewrite with your blog in mind. Consider possibilties for a weekly column—something you're interested in sharing, such as writing rituals, what you're reading, or the progress of your current project. Don't just think in terms of words but think visually as well—in what ways do images inspire you, and how can you use imagery to inspire readers? By thinking of what motivates you to write—from literary quotes to a fantastic new novel—share what you know and love.

Fifteen-minute marketing: Whenever you think you don't have the time write a blog post, give yourself fifteen minutes, and post whatever you finish in that amount of time. It's better to have more frequent, shorter posts than fewer, very long posts—many blog readers skim, and it makes sense to keep your blog more active with good, short bits than to post infrequently when your readers may not get through an entire post anyway. Divide your fifteen minutes of blog-writing time into three five-minute sections: First, write a very rough draft. Next, add visuals, links, or anything else that might enhance your post. Finally, polish and proofread it—and then you're done.

Everyday marketing: Just as you're always thinking like a writer in your everyday life (i.e., seeing everything as possible material), think this way as a blogger, too. Notice the world around you in ways that might result in a blog post, whether you witness something interesting that relates to something in your book, or whether you read a news article set in the same country as your novel. Readers also enjoy learning about the behind-the-scenes lives of their favorite authors, especially if there's some special expertise you have that ties in with your book (for example, if you're a lawyer writing legal thrillers, or a journalist writing crime fiction), so writing about your daily life can be great blog material.

DEVELOP A MAILING LIST

It may sound a little salesy, but having a mailing list is a great way to keep your friends, family, and colleagues in the loop—not to mention new readers and anyone you meet who may be interested in your book. The nice thing about a mailing list is that it's one more way to reach out; for example, you likely have some Facebook friends who go months without logging in, but you'll still want to make sure they receive your e-mail news about a book giveaway or an upcoming event.

You'll begin with family and close friends; then ask colleagues and more casual acquaintances whether you may add them to your mailing list. Don't forget about former classmates (from grade school to grad school), writing buddies (from your writing group to those you've met at conferences), the parents of your kids' friends, and so on. (Note that you should always get permission from the recipient before adding anyone to your list.) And, whenever you do a reading or any other event, pass around a guest book or a simple sign-up sheet so that readers can sign up to receive your mailings.

If your list grows long, you'll want to be sure to send out e-mails in small batches (twenty recipients or so) to avoid being targeted for spamming—and of course, always blind-cc the recipients to preserve their privacy. Once your list does grow longer, consider signing up for an e-mail service (I like Mail Chimp, which has free options and plenty of easy-to-use templates; Mad Mimi and Campaign Monitor are also popular). These programs allow you to design nice announcements about your book launch and other events; you can also do more lengthy e-newsletters if you have a lot to share.

Here are few more pointers for e-mail marketing...

Be clear about what you'll be sending.

When people sign up for something, they like to know what it is, so don't hide the fact that you'll be sending out updates on your book; even if it sounds promotional, you need to manage expectations (and see below for how to do more than simply promote yourself). Also, be sure to let subscribers know that you won't be sharing their e-mail addresses with anyone else; maintaining the privacy of those who trust you with their e-mail addresses is important.

Don't send e-mails too frequently.

If, for example, you're a teacher and hold frequent events, you might send out a regular e-newsletter, as long as the information is relevant to its recipients. But if you're simply sending out announcements about the occasional event or new review, be a little more restrained; sending out too many e-mails with too little content (or content that is solely self-promotional) may cause people to stop reading or unsubscribe. Also, these e-mail campaigns take valuable time to create, so you'll want to use this time wisely. I recommend sending out monthly e-mails if you have a lot of news to share; otherwise, send e-mails four to eight times a year, depending on what news you have. Either way, try to be consistent, so that no one hears from you too often but so they don't think you've dropped off the face of the earth, either.

Create different lists.

This can take a lot of time initially, but it's very valuable in the end. For example, if you're a New York City writer with an e-mail list of 1,000 recipients all over the country, and you're doing a series of events in New York, not everyone needs to receive an e-mail about these events. When you pass out a guest book or sign-up sheet, ask people to add their locations so that you can better target your audience.

Offer a little more than promotion.

While the purpose of the e-mail may be to promote your book, offer a little something more as well—recipients may tire of the content if it's always the same and always about you. For my own newsletter for writers (which I send out four to six times a year), I include a writing tip and a writing prompt, so that among the promotional stuff there will always be something for writers in there. I also try to add things that may be helpful for writers, from links about publishing to writing software I've discovered. You can also include links to other writers, blogs, and websites that you think your audience will enjoy—and consider offering book giveaways or other bonuses to your subscribers.

Be friendly and personal.

One mistake I made when I first started sending out e-newsletters was trying to sound formal and extremely professional. Then I noticed, having received a number of such e-mails myself, that this is a little boring and impersonal. So now I try to sound casual and accessible, and I keep mailings short and to the point. You should always show how readers can unsubscribe if they'd like to, and it's a great idea to invite feedback and comments. And always proofread your e-mail before sending it. Typos happen, but I usually create a campaign at least a week in advance so I can put it aside, then look at it again with fresh eyes before scheduling it.

Use pictures.

Visuals are great for e-mail campaigns; no one wants to wade through a ton of text, and most people simply skim through e-mail announcements or newsletters anyway, so you'll want a mix of text and images to help keep readers' attention. You must, of course, own the rights to any photo you use—an exception is your book cover, which you'll be allowed to use for marketing purposes, so you might consider having a banner highlighting the title and/or some of the cover design; think of it as your logo. (If you have more than one book, you can use the most recent one, or use something from your website that will familiarize readers with you as an author.)

Don't over-design.

While you want to be visually appealing, don't make the mistake of going crazy with too many images (which could be distracting) or fancy fonts (which could be hard to read). Choose a template that is easy on the eyes, with plenty of white space to make it skimmable and reader friendly. Strive for simple and engaging.

Make use of the tools.

If you use an e-mail marketing service, check out the tools it offers for tracking who opens your e-mails, which links are most popular, etc. You can also experiment with sending your news out at different times of day and different times of the week to see what the best results are. Nowadays, e-mail services allow you to connect your campaigns with social media, so you can link your e-news with Twitter or Facebook if you'd like. It's worth spending a little time on these to gauge the effects of your marketing efforts and to plan your next campaign accordingly.

Don't worry about the "unsubscribes."

One thing I love about Mail Chimp is the little note that comes along with the notification that someone has just unsubscribed from my list: "Maybe they're just not into you?" This never fails to make me smile, which is important when someone has just unsubscribed. I find myself worrying about all sorts of things: Was my e-mail too boring? Was it something I said? Did they read my book and hate it? The fact is, people are overwhelmed with e-mail, and it's likely not personal (and if it is, there's not much you can do about it anyway, so it's best not to fret over it). Most often, I suspect, people unsubscribe for reasons having more to do with their own lives than with the content of your e-mail.

Everyday Marketing Tips

Thirty-minute marketing: Plan to spend some time exploring e-mail services, and ask fellow writers what services they use and what the pros and cons are. You'll want to explore costs (many services are free but only up to a certain number of recipients), ease of use, design templates, and more before signing up. If you're the recipient of any e-mail newsletters yourself, save them in a file to study them later and help you decide which e-mail service to choose.

Everyday marketing: When you meet new people (or run into old friends), ask if they'd like to hear from you regarding your book and upcoming events—and get their e-mail addresses. You don't want to be pushy, of course, but if someone expresses a genuine interest in what you do, this is a great opportunity to ask. As soon as you have a plan for your book's publication (contract, release date, etc.), begin collecting names and e-mail addresses (keeping them in an Excel spreadsheet makes importing them easy) so you'll be ready when you begin your first mailing.

More everyday marketing: Always remember that visuals are important for mailings—so keep a camera and/or smartphone handy to photograph anything that might make a nice visual for your next newsletter, whether it's a vintage typewriter, a literary-looking café, or just a tranquil scene in a park. It's a good idea to have plenty of visuals on hand, and much better to use your own—stock photos tend to look bland and generic, and at least your own photos will have little stories behind them.

SET UP GOOGLE ALERTS

If you don't already have a Google account, you'll need one to set up alerts. Setting up alerts is very straightforward (it's right on the Google menu once you have an account set up), and it's great for keeping up on your own news. Set up an alert for your name and your book title, as well as any other topics that may be relevant to your book. Then, according to how you adjust your settings, you'll be notified (daily, weekly, or whenever) as your name comes up (on websites, blogs, in the news, etc.).

JOIN AND BE ACTIVE ON SOCIAL NETWORKS

There are so many social networks these days, I can hardly keep track. And the popularity of one site today may be entirely different in a year, or even in a month. So you'll have to explore these sites, be active and flexible, and evolve.

Facebook, Twitter, and Goodreads are excellent networks for writers (see below for specific tips on how best to use each of these as an author). Pinterest can be great for writers with visually oriented books (illustrated children's books, cookbooks, and design books, to name a few examples). Other sites I've joined are LinkedIn, She Writes (for women writers), LibraryThing, Shelfari, and Red Room. Not all of these will be useful for all authors—and there are sure to be more out there by the time you read this—so take a look, see what you think, and sign up for those networks that you think will be useful to you. All of these resources are currently free, but what they do cost you is time—so join only the networks that you're able to spend time on and that will allow you to make good connections.

Facebook for authors

When I learned, back in 2008, that my first book would be published, I didn't even have a Facebook account. (I was also the last person on the planet to get an answering machine in the eighties and the last person to get a cell phone in the nineties.) In general, I prefer solitude, or being with people face-to-face. So it was with great reluctance that I signed up for Facebook, which, as most writers know, seems non-negotiable if you have a book out in the world that you actually want people to read. (That said, I do know a number of successful writers who are not on Facebook, so if you truly hate the idea, stay true to yourself ... but do be aware that it offers a lot of wonderful opportunities.)

To my own surprise, I discovered that, even for someone who likes her solitude and face time, it wasn't difficult to get hooked on Facebook. It can be seriously addictive. The good news for writers is that for at least part of the time you're on Facebook, you're doing legitimate work. The bad news is that the rest of the time, you're not—and you have to balance this Facebook time with writing your next book, with not ignoring your family, and with your day job.

Here are some Facebook tips to help you achieve that balance.

Set up a book or author page.

If you set up a separate book or author page, you won't need to combine your author life with your personal life. (See below for more on privacy issues.) This will allow readers you don't know to "Like" your page while allowing you to keep your regular Facebook page (and the photos of your kids or your last high school reunion) private. Also, while there is a limit to the number of Facebook friends you can have, there's no limit to the number of people who can "Like" your book or author page, so you can keep building your audience indefinitely.

If you have a book or author page, Facebook allows you to "use Facebook as X," and from there, you can "Like" other pages that may be relevant to your book, such as a travel website or a bookstore. Having a separate page also allows you to post book updates for those who want to see them rather than for your entire network of Facebook friends and family, some of whom may be less interested in your writing than others (sad but true). Having started out with a FORGETTING ENGLISH book page (I thought at the time I might never publish another book), I eventually had to launch a MIDGE RAYMOND—AUTHOR page once I published a second book. This left me with two pages and a divided audience—not ideal, to say the least. So, I recommend an author page over a book page, simply because if and when you publish your next book, you won't have to start a new page, and you won't have two separate audiences.

Make friends.

Facebook is a great way to reconnect with old friends, colleagues, and acquaintances. And Facebook provides an even better way to stay connected to new people you meet at readings and conferences (who needs business cards anymore?).

So do be open to friend requests from fellow writers, readers, and others—but be sure to accept friend requests only from people you know or want to know (you can always un-friend them later, of course, but this is very awkward). Reach out and connect with readers and writers yourself; include a personal message if it's someone you don't know well, or someone who may need to be reminded of where he or she met you. And once you make new friends, be sure to invite them to "Like" your book or author page—even if you don't spring it on them immediately, be sure to do this eventually.

Don't be overly promotional.

This is the quickest way to get hidden or un-friended. I'm sure I've been guilty of this on occasion—it's hard not to be enthusiastic when your book first launches or when a great new review comes out—but you always have to balance this with the danger of becoming boring, or annoying, or worse. Be sure you don't simply use Facebook to blast your own news but to engage—comment on others' updates; share their good news along with your own.

Use images.

Facebook is great for posting images of your book and photos from events (and *always* try to get photos from events, whether it's a reading or a book club meeting), and you can use this opportunity not only to post a photo but to thank your event host(s) as well.

Don't offer too much information.

Readers love getting glimpses into writers' lives—to a point. You'll definitely want to show your personal side, but stay focused on offering readers a little more than they can get from the bio on your book cover without taking away all the mystery or freaking them out with details they may not want to know about you.

Be respectful.

If you want to attract a wide audience for your book, carefully consider political rants or offbeat humor posts before posting them. It's not that you shouldn't be who you are—you should, especially if you have strong opinions that define you; again, readers love getting to know writers—but just keep in mind that what you say affects how you're perceived.

Keep your social media posts separate.

Different forms of social media are, and should be, used in different ways (see below for some tips on how to use Twitter, which is very different from Facebook). Some believe that everything should be networked—that your blog posts and tweets and status updates should all be connected—but in fact, this can be counterproductive in that your followers/ friends are then inundated with every single update in every format possible. And sometimes—especially around book-launch time when you're in promotion mode—this can be too much, and you may be hidden or un-friended by the very people you hope to engage. So while it may take a little extra time, don't bombard all your accounts at once with every bit of information you want to disseminate; keep everything you share as relevant to its intended audience as possible, and your connections will be more engaged.

Be active.

This doesn't mean spending all your time on Facebook, but it does mean you'll want to be active enough to give meaning to the "social" in "social network." Before, during, and just after your book launch, check your Facebook page at least a couple times a day; update your status once or twice a day; respond to all posts and engage as much as you can during this important time. Then, after the book launch, try setting yourself a schedule—a half an hour in the morning, a half an hour at night; twenty minutes a day; one day a week—something that allows you to stay active but not totally immersed.

Keep in mind that less is usually more.

Posting one or two status updates per day may not sound like much, but too many posts every day, day after day, could get you hidden or un-friended by a great many of the people you're trying to reach. Aim to keep posts and links fun, relevant, and interesting to increase the likelihood of them being read. And every so often, take a look at your posts to see what works best—for example, how many views, likes, comments, and shares you get when you post on a weekday versus a weekend? Do people tend to respond when you post more often, or less often? Results are different for everyone, so while Facebook is meant to be social and fun, it's also a great promotional tool, so see what works for you as an author and your own personal network.

Safeguard your privacy, as well as that of your friends and family.

Facebook gets a lot of bad publicity when it comes to privacy issues, but in fact, it's often the users themselves who offer up more information than Facebook does. The first line of defense is to avoid becoming friends with anyone you don't know personally—but of course this isn't realistic for authors trying to promote books; the goal is to reach out and connect with readers everywhere. So you may be opening up your Facebook profile to a lot of strangers—most of whom will be wonderful people, some of whom may not be.

Here are a few good rules to go by in terms of protecting your privacy while being open to connecting with readers:

- Do not include on your Facebook profile anything that can be used to access any of your personal information. For starters, don't use the same password for Facebook that you use for banking, work, healthcare accounts, etc. And if you use your pet's name as a password, don't mention said pet's name on Facebook. Avoid including anything that a stranger can't find on your website or blog. While this will exclude many of the things that make Facebook fun, think about it—the passwords you use and/or security questions you answer to access your bank and other important accounts usually have to do with things only you will know (supposedly). So consider this before you share it all online.

- Adjust your settings to keep certain things private: your e-mail, your phone number, your address; any of these can be used to hack into a bank account either by phone or online.

- Disable the feature that "checks you in"—which essentially means that everyone on Facebook knows exactly where you are when you post. If you're on a book tour, naturally you'll be posting about that— but do keep in mind that all of your connections will then know you're out of town and for how long. Again, avoid putting your address anywhere, especially if your place will be empty while you're away. And while you're at it, you might also mention that you have a big, hulking neighbor keeping an eye on your home while he's dog-sitting your six Dobermans.

- Enable https, which you'll find under Account Security—this enables secure browsing and will help prevent your account from being hacked into (surely I'm not the only one who's gotten e-mails from friends saying, "Sorry, that nasty video wasn't from me..."). This is especially important if you're using an open wireless network or a public computer to log in.

- Take care with apps and games. For increased privacy, one thing you'll want to do is uncheck the boxes in the Info Available to Applications setting— Facebook encourages you to check all the boxes, saying "the more you share, the more social the experience," when in fact, the more you share, the more vulnerable you are. Even those games people seem to enjoy so much on Facebook, like "25 Things About Me," can reveal information that you don't want the wrong people to have. Share only what you don't mind the whole world knowing, just in case.

All that said, don't be so paranoid that you don't have fun on Facebook—in fact, the most fun for me isn't necessarily the ability to share but the ability to chat with others and to enjoy their photos and news. And perhaps this is the best way to view social media, especially as an author who uses Facebook in part for book promotion: to remember that while it's a great way to get the word out, it's less about self-promotion than about the give-and-take.

Everyday Marketing Tips

Thirty-minute marketing: Whether you already use Facebook for fun or you're joining reluctantly, limit yourself to thirty minutes per day. If you have a slight addiction, hop on three times a day for only ten minutes at a time—if you can take it or leave it, log on once a day. You might find that fifteen minutes at the beginning of the day and at the end is a nice balance—it allows you to post an update, browse a bit, and then log off until later, when you can respond to any comments you've received, post again, and enjoy a few more friends' posts.

Everyday marketing: Whenever you're on Facebook, think of it as work time as well as play time. You'll want to engage as you usually do, but also think about what sort of updates most intrigue you and how you can replicate these when it comes to your book—for example, how can you use visuals to make your updates more fun and less overtly promotional? How can you ask the right questions to engage your Facebook friends without being salesy?

Twitter for authors

The social network Twitter allows people to follow one another and receive and post messages of 140 characters or fewer. It isn't as interactive or visual as Facebook (though you can post photos) and is best used for posting little bits of information, particularly links: to an event, to a new blog post, to a new review, etc.

I admit to being late to Twitter. I just didn't get it. I didn't get why I should be, or how anyone else could be, interested in 140-character updates about people's lives. But then my book was published, and everything changed. Not only have I "joined the conversation," as they say, but I also manage several Twitter accounts (my own, and four for the day job), and I use a time-saver called HootSuite (more on this later).

When it comes to book promotion, Twitter is great for some things, not great for others. And I have to admit that, as anyone who first followed me @MidgeRaymond knows, my Twitter personality suffered a bit of a dissociative identity disorder. Translation: I was (and sometimes still am) all over the place. I tweet mostly about books, publishing, writing, about my writer friends and what they're up to, as well as other random stuff. One thing I learned with Twitter is that people like to follow you for a specific reason—for example, they're fellow writers, or they love to read. So in an effort to be more focused, I've worked on narrowing my Twitter life down to tweeting about all things bookish—and it not only saves me time but gives my followers the content they're interested in, which is why they began following me in the first place.

Twitter can be a lot of work initially, and it takes some time to build a network, but it will allow you to connect with readers, writers, and bloggers, and it's a very accessible way to find people with similar interests. So how can a writer best use Twitter?

First, choose an account name that fits your goals. You might use your name, as I do, or you might use the title of your book—but keep in mind that if you publish more than one book, you'll then need to have more than one Twitter feed. And don't forget to upload a photo; you'll want to offer the sense of a real person behind your tweets in order to find your audience.

Next, once your account is set up, start tweeting. Be sure that your first tweets offer a little bit of what you're about without being too self-promotional (see below for more). Try to keep these first tweets especially engaging and informative.

Then, find people with similar interests, news, and information to share—and follow them. As soon as you begin to follow people, you'll find that most of these people follow you back, and then you're all receiving and transmitting tweets—and you've officially "joined the conversation."

Note: Take your time. If you follow zillions of people at once, you'll be overwhelmed by the number of tweets coming your way and won't be able to process anything. (You also might look a little nutty if you're following 10,000 people and only have 2 followers yourself.) So take your time, check out what people are talking about, and engage. Only follow people and organizations you are truly interested in, and if someone follows you, follow him or her back only if you really want to; otherwise, you'll be overwhelmed and less able to use Twitter to actually connect. Also, avoid asking people to follow you in return for your following them—this only seems desperate. (The one exception—feel free to let friends, family, and colleagues know about your new Twitter account and invite them to follow you.)

Getting started requires quite a lot of initial hanging out on Twitter, but by taking the time, you'll learn what makes interesting tweets (basically by noting which ones you read and which you don't) and what all those cryptic little abbreviations mean (RT for retweet, #FF for Follow Friday, the #hashtag that makes for easy searches for such terms as #writer or #fiction). You'll learn how a reply is different from a direct message, and that it's polite to credit someone whose link you're retweeting.

And of course, as you're learning all this, you'll be tweeting the whole time yourself. So, what to tweet?

There are plenty of "rules" about Twitter, but I don't believe we can, or need to, try to follow them religiously (mostly because everyone has an opinion on it, and the "rules" change accordingly). So tweet about what's interesting to you, and be as focused or as loose as you'd like—the most important thing is that you say something tweet-worthy. Here are a few guidelines.

Be user friendly.

Include a photo (your book cover is also fine, especially around launch time, but keep in mind that people like to see the face behind the tweets). Also, make your bio count—Twitter requires that it's short, but make sure you include all the relevant info, most importantly the title of your book and your website's URL.

Be relevant.

Offer content that your followers can use; don't just tweet about what you had for breakfast. Offer links to interesting articles and blogs; offer writing exercises and tips that have helped you; offer quotes by famous authors. Use hashtags to be part of a larger conversation (#NaNoWriMo, for example, if you participate in National Novel Writing Month). You'll want to tweet not only things your followers will enjoy reading but things that they'll be inspired to retweet as well.

Be interesting.

I could also rephrase this as "Don't over-promote." Even if you're on Twitter to promote your book, if *every* tweet is all about you and your book, that's going to bore people quickly. There's absolutely nothing wrong with showing off a good review or tweeting about an upcoming event—but be sure to produce some other content as well.

Include links.

To me, this is the most useful aspect of Twitter—discovering articles, events, photos, videos, and other tidbits that I haven't already seen or read. There's only so much you can do in 140 characters, and I find that the most useful, interesting, and entertaining tweets usually have a link or a photo attached (and, as you'll find out quickly, you'll need to use a link shortener like bit.ly or Tinyurl).

Network.

Follow people and organizations that interest you, which will allow you to start to build a network. Always do your best to respond to direct messages (unless they're only blatant sales pitches, which often they are) and follow people back when they follow you (again, only if they are of interest to you; some of them won't be).

Try out the tools.

It wasn't until I had more than one Twitter account that I tried HootSuite, and I love it. By scheduling my tweets in advance, I can space out a day's worth of tweets without being tied to the computer all day, and I can also tweet even when I'm nowhere near a computer. HootSuite also makes it easy to manage all my Twitter accounts from one place. There are a great many Twitter tools out there—so many it's a little overwhelming—but they are worth knowing about, so do a little research and see if any of them can help save you time and stay organized.

Be generous.

Even though I originally joined Twitter with my own book promotion in mind, I use Twitter to promote writer friends' events, to link to their blogs, to show off their work. Twitter is not just about throwing your own thoughts (or book reviews, or what you're making for dinner) out there; it's meant to be a conversation, and when it works well, it truly is. As an example, one cool way writers can find great stories as well as promote other writers is with #StorySunday, originated by The Short Review, in which readers link to their favorite online short story of the week. You can also use #FF (Follow Friday) or #WW (Writer Wednesday) to share other writers' blogs and websites. Always thank those who do this for you, which you can do via a reply on Twitter, and be sure to credit those whose tweets you share. Also, when you mention others, don't forget to use their Twitter handle—@MidgeRaymond, for example—so that they'll know you mentioned them and so that others can find and follow them.

Have fun. Be creative. Think outside the newsy tweet. Enjoy.

But while you're being creative, take care not to be so "out there" as to lose followers (see **Be relevant**, above). And remember to stay under 140 characters, and then some; it's best to leave a little room for people to comment and retweet what you post.

Keep a balance.

Another important thing to keep in mind is how much time being an active Twitter user takes. To be fully engaged, you really have to spend some time reading tweets, interacting, replying, retweeting, and so forth—when you would probably rather be (and should be) writing. So once you've got yourself oriented on Twitter, allow yourself an allotted amount of daily Twitter time, and then get back to work. Using HootSuite or other tools allows you to tweet consistently without being tied to the network all day.

Manage your follows.

Another way you'll want to stay balanced is in terms of followers. If you follow far more people than are following you, take a look at those you follow and determine whether you really need to follow them. And then try to figure out why you're not getting more followers yourself: Are you being too self-promotional? In what ways can you make your content more engaging or relevant? You can also use a tool like Manage Flitter to see who is following you back, who is active or inactive on Twitter, and other information that will make assessing your own account helpful.

And, finally, how do you know if any of it is "working"? You can attempt to measure your success in book sales or in the number of followers you have, or you can check out your "Twitter influence" with such tools as Klout. But keep in mind that for a writer, success may mean something that's not quantifiable—such as how much you're learning and sharing, or how well you're staying connected to the online writing community. I suggest defining your own goals and measuring your success from there.

Everyday Marketing Tips

Ten-minute marketing: Whenever you have about ten minutes to spare, log on to Twitter with one short goal in mind, and tweet away. For example: Do a hashtag search on a keyword related to your book (or simply #writing, #novel, #writer, etc.). Peruse what's out there, and share interesting tweets; come up with something of your own to add. Another example: Take a moment to promote a friend's recent book review or event. Create a list of simple, quick Twitter opportunities like these and fire off a few tweets whenever you have a couple moments to spare.

Everyday marketing: As you read the local and national news—even as you read your favorite magazines or literary journals—look for stories, photos, book reviews, etc., that you can share with your Twitter followers. Always keep in mind that it needs to be interesting, relevant, and something you yourself would enjoy reading.

Goodreads

Goodreads is a website for readers on which books are listed and reviewed. You may already have a Goodreads account; if so, apply to become a Goodreads Author (see below). Over the years, various studies have shown that word of mouth is the way most people choose the books they read—and this is what Goodreads provides, only virtually.

Here are few tips for getting involved and making the most of Goodreads.

First, become a Goodreads Author.

Once you've signed up with Goodreads, you then have to let Goodreads know that your book is your book. It's a simple process—you look up your title, then let Goodreads know that this title is written by you. It usually takes a day or so for Goodreads to verify this.

Next, fill out your personal profile.

As with Facebook, you'll want to choose carefully what you share—but do include your author bio, as well as a link to your website and Twitter account. If you have a blog, you can connect your blog feed to your Goodreads profile (a very good way to expand your reach). And don't forget to include a photo.

Invite your friends—and make new ones.

Many of your friends and family members may already be on Goodreads, so be sure to connect with them—then invite those who haven't yet discovered Goodreads. By inviting your friends, you can not only introduce them to Goodreads but also create your own virtual book group. Because your friends are likely to be among your biggest fans, encourage them to rate, review, and chat about your book with their network of friends. Also, reach out and connect with new readers.

Be active as a reader as well as an author.

Goodreads members have created myriad types of book groups—join them as a reader to get a feel for how they work, and the more engaged you become, the more you'll be able to find groups that might be interested in your book. Become "a fan" of your favorite authors, and keep adding, rating, and reviewing the books you're reading.

Do a book giveaway (or two).

Book giveaways are allowed within the first six months of a book's release, and there's some flexibility there—for example, you can do one giveaway for two copies of your book, or two giveaways for one copy each. Presumably, whoever wins your book will read it and write a Goodreads review—but even if this doesn't happen, what will happen is that your book will be added to many, many virtual bookshelves, and this is great exposure. I recommend doing more than one giveaway, spaced at least a month apart, which will help keep the buzz going. And when you schedule your giveaway, schedule the end date at least three to four weeks from the start date, so people will have a chance to discover your book and sign up to win. And when you do mail out that free copy, include a warm note to the lucky recipient asking for a review if he or she enjoys the book.

Make a list.

Add to existing lists. Listopia is a mini-site that includes lists upon lists upon lists. Whether you write YA fiction or memoir, you'll have plenty to choose from. Lists are great ways to make your book more discoverable to others—and to discover books yourself.

A few other sites to consider...

She Writes

This is a virtual network for women writers, where you can set up a profile, join groups, invite friends, read articles, list events, and more. It's for writers only, not necessarily readers, but it's great for finding likeminded souls and for sharing ideas on everything from events to writing to promotion. For promotional opportunities, check out submission guidelines for the She Writes Blog.

LibraryThing

This site is another community for book lovers. Here you can create a profile and add a photo and links to your website, blog, your publisher's website, and all your social media accounts.

Shelfari

Like Goodreads and LibraryThing, this is a community of readers. It includes reviews, communities, and groups.

Red Room

This site is for both authors and readers. You can create a profile, upload blog posts, join groups, etc.

Everyday Marketing Tips

Thirty-minute marketing: All social networks require a bit of commitment, but with so many different aspects of book promotion requiring your attention, be sure to limit your time on these networks. Aim for spending no more than thirty minutes a day—fewer, if possible. And split up these thirty minutes to keep any social media addiction in check. Log on for shorter times at various times of day; also, divide your time among networks—of your thirty minutes, spend ten minutes on Twitter, for example, and twenty minutes on Goodreads; or spend fifteen minutes on Facebook and another fifteen on Twitter. Vary it day by day, with a thirty-minute limit.

Everyday marketing: Use apps so that you can log in to your social networks for quick updates while you're otherwise stuck somewhere, like standing in line at the DMV or waiting for your kid's soccer practice to end. Always make the most of these moments of "wasted time," which can really add up.

SET UP A BOOK TOUR

The first stop—a book launch party

A book launch party is a great way to celebrate the release of your book—and it's an even better way to introduce your book to those who will be among your biggest supporters: friends, family, colleagues, etc.

Many authors choose to use a public venue for a book launch party—a bookstore or library, for example—and this is also a good idea in that it will ensure you have a decent crowd at your first public event. But consider hosting a private book launch party as well, either before or after your first public reading—for one, you'll probably find that anyone who can't attend one event will come to the other; two, the events are different enough that many of the same people may attend both.

A private book launch party is meant to be more intimate than a reading—it's a party, after all. It's a chance to celebrate with those closest to you in a setting where you'll actually be able to chat with people (this is often difficult, if not impossible, at a public reading). And, if anyone really wants to hear you read, they can come out to one of your public events as well.

You can host your launch party yourself, at someone's home, or even at a local restaurant or pub. Here are a few tips for creating a fun launch:

- Make it festive, and aim to have the food, drink, decorations, and music reflect your book in some way.

- Send printed invitations or Evites, and ask everyone invited to bring a friend (or two) along. Let people know your book will be available if they don't have it yet; if they do, remind them to bring it along for you to sign.

- Have plenty of books available and enlist someone to handle selling them for you—a book launch party is among the better sales opportunities for the first-time published author (especially if there is wine involved!). Those who are proudest of you will purchase a signed copy not only for themselves but for friends and family members as well. Have your sales representative remind everyone that books make excellent gifts for all occasions.

- Make it easy for people to purchase your book— be ready to make change, accept checks, and take credit cards using Square or PayPal.

- Keep a pen handy to sign books—and try to think of a few good ideas for inscriptions beforehand (as writers, we're supposed to be good at this, but I always find myself having no idea what to write). You'll want each inscription to be personal, of course, but thinking of ways in which to express your gratitude, affection, etc., beforehand helps a lot when you've got a line of people waiting for their books to be signed.

- Have plenty of postcards, bookmarks, etc., available for partygoers to take with them so they can share them among their own circles.

Onward—embarking on a more public book tour

Forgetting English came out twice—once from Eastern Washington University Press, after winning the Spokane Prize for Short Fiction—and again, from Press 53, after EWU Press closed its doors. On one hand, it was awful to have my publisher shut down and leave me out of print—on the other, I got to have a second book tour, with an updated edition of my book and a spiffy new cover.

Among the best things I learned from doing two book tours for the same book, two years apart, is that The Book Tour comes in so many different shapes and forms. And the most important thing for any author to know is which type of tour will work best, for both the writer and the book.

The old days of publisher-sponsored, multi-city book tours are, for the most part, long gone. These days, the vast majority of authors must plan, pay for, and publicize their own book tours—which is no small task. And for writers who don't have a background in publishing, publicity, or marketing, it can seem even more intimidating.

But the challenges are well worth it, as the rewards can be great. Keeping in mind the nature of your book, your schedule, and your budget, here are a few things to consider as you begin to think about planning a tour that will best fit your needs.

Go where your friends are.

Choose venues that you know will draw a decent audience, i.e., always plan book tour stops and events in places where you know at least a few people who will show up, bring friends, and otherwise make sure you'll have a nice showing.

If you're doing mostly local or regional events, spread them out so that the venues aren't competing with one another. When *Forgetting English* first came out in 2009, I was living in Seattle, where I did about a dozen book events—but I spread them out over the course of the year, so no one got too sick of me and the venues didn't have to compete for customers since even similar events were spaced months apart.

Team up with a fellow writer.

For my 2011 tour, I teamed up for many events with my friend and colleague Wendy Call, author of *No Word for Welcome*. Because our books have similar themes (both are about foreign locales, though mine is fiction and Wendy's is nonfiction), we thought it would be great to offer joint events, with something for all readers, and we received enthusiastic responses from booksellers, community writing centers, and libraries. Best of all, we shared the workload (the cold calls, follow-ups, and creation of marketing materials) as well as the fun stuff (great events, great people, lots of wine). Even better, we could commiserate over the not-so-fun stuff (the rejections, the small crowds, the low book sales). In all, it was a wonderful experience and one I'm so glad to have shared with Wendy. So if your book is a good fit with another writer's, consider setting up a few joint events, which can offer a great way to share the experience as well as broaden your audience.

Think outside the bookstore.

Certain times of year (holidays, for example, or summer in the Pacific Northwest) can be nearly impossible for scheduling bookstore events. And sometimes, no matter what the time of year, a bookstore may be booked already, or your schedules won't align. So always be thinking beyond the bookstore—

you'll not only find gems in new venues but discover whole new audiences as well.

Libraries, for example, are always open to author events, particularly if the author is local and there's an educational component to your book or presentation. Also, look for community centers or literary centers such as The Loft Literary Center in Minneapolis, Grub Street in Boston, Richard Hugo House in Seattle, or San Diego Writers Ink in San Diego. Among the places I've read or attended readings are museums and galleries, cafés, universities and colleges, book clubs, historical societies … the list is endless if you think about it, so get a little creative.

If your book is nonfiction, this in and of itself can help you find good venues (if you've written a book with an environmental theme, for example, seek out organizations that embrace this theme and see how you can help one another). And fiction writers, too, should look for the same opportunities; simply use your fictional characters and settings in nonfictional ways. If your protagonist is an artist, hold an event at a local arts center or in an artist's studio; if your book is set in Thailand, host an event at a Thai restaurant; if your main character is a barista, get readers together at a local café.

You might also ask someone you know to host a literary salon—a great way to find new readers and talk about your book in a more private, casual setting. Ask a friend (even someone in another city/state, where you'll be able to reach out to new readers) to host a salon for you at his or her home. Bring copies of the book to sell; provide whatever food, wine, etc., you'd like at the event. Then simply plan a casual gathering around your book, which might include a brief reading, discussion, and Q&A.

Research book festivals and conferences around the country, and see which ones you might attend as a reader, presenter, or instructor. Book festivals and conferences are wonderful ways to reach new readers—all have built-in literary audiences, and it's also a great way to connect with fellow authors. Keep in mind that most festivals and conferences schedule up to a year in advance, so be sure to do your research early.

Offer a little something more.

Unless you're a writer whose mere presence in a bookstore will guarantee a line out the door, think about offering a little more than a traditional reading/signing. You want the event to be a win-win (so that you not only find new readers but will be invited back enthusiastically when you publish your next book), so think beyond your book to what else you can offer. Because *Forgetting English* is set in eight countries across four continents, for many of my events I offered a travel-writing workshop, which brings in not only readers but writers and travelers as well. So even if no one's ever heard of me or my writing (which is, in fact, most people), those who love to travel or write will show up to learn something—and one of the things they learn is what my book is all about. On our joint tour, Wendy and I held several mini-workshops, and we received terrific feedback from these events. Even if an event isn't specifically about your book, you're giving participants an opportunity to get to know you, which in turn will build interest in your work.

Try a virtual book tour.

This is a great option of you don't have the time or budget to do a traditional book tour. You'll do many of the same things you'd do on a live, in-person tour—create buzz for your book, find new readers, and chat about your book. Keep in mind that, while virtual, this type of book tour still takes a lot of planning: You need to connect with host bloggers, come up with original topics to write about, and promote your tour. See page 84 for more about virtual book tours.

Events are all about the details...

Here are a few pre–book launch tips for planning events—and see Part 3 for launch-time tips and details (such as how to give a good reading and a pre-event checklist).

Plan in advance!

Bookstores and libraries generally schedule from three to six months in advance—always give the venue a call to see when you'll need to send a proposal in order to be considered for an event. There's always a chance you can get in at a later date, especially if you're a local author, but I definitely recommend advance planning, especially if you have certain venues in mind.

Libraries often host themed events—around holidays, for example, and especially during the summer—so call in advance to see what their summer theme will be and whether you might be a good fit.

Ask all sorts of questions.

If you're reading at a bookstore, ask whether the staff member who will be there would like you to provide an introduction (most booksellers will write one up, but every so often this doesn't happen, and it's incredibly awkward when a bookseller doesn't introduce you well, or at all). So always offer to provide an intro—anything that saves a busy bookseller time will be much appreciated. A good intro should be about a paragraph long (something that can be read in less than one minute) and should include a little about you and a little about the book, including (especially!) any awards it has received as well as quotes from good reviews. (See Nan Macy's Q&A on page 229 for more on bookstore events.)

If you're reading at a library, ask whether you will be able to sell books (some libraries don't allow this). If you're not allowed to sell books, however, this doesn't mean you shouldn't schedule an event—it still may be well worth your while to reach these new readers. Simply pass out bookmarks or other materials with your book info, making it clear where readers can find your book if they want to read it, including the library at which you're presenting. (See Amy Blossom's Q&A on page 224 for more on planning library events.)

If you'd like to make it festive, ask the venue whether you can provide refreshments, decorations, or anything else that might make your event more fun. Most libraries aren't allowed to serve alcohol, but you might be able to bring wine to a bookstore or gallery.

Promote, promote, promote.

Once your events are set up, the real work begins. Again, a happy experience for all involved is when you have a nice crowd and when you sell books. And you can't count on the venue to do all the promotion for you—this is your job as well. Below is a list of the minimum you should plan to do for any event.

- Use social media to promote your events, beginning a month in advance.

- Create postcards, bookmarks, and/or flyers to offer to venues.

- List your events on your website, and ask venues for their local media lists so that you can send press releases and/or calendar announcements.

- Send out invitations (by mail, e-mail, or Evite) to those you know in the area, inviting them to come and bring friends along.

Enjoy, enjoy, enjoy.

Remember that this is fun. (Really, it is.) The process of setting up all these events can be both exhilarating and exhausting—and running around to all of them can be even more so. This is when it's important to remember why you're doing all this: You've published your book. You're getting it out there in the world. And you're meeting your readers. For a writer, what could be better than that?

Give thanks to all.

Don't forget to thank everyone who made your tour possible, from the independent bookstores to your salon hosts to the readers who showed up to support your book. And even more important, hold on to this spirit of gratitude—it'll make your entire book tour lots of fun, even in the challenging moments.

Everyday Marketing Tips

Thirty-minute marketing: In order to properly schedule events, you'll need to do some planning: create a proposal, follow up by e-mail and by phone, and work out the details with the event coordinator of the venue. During the four to six months before your book release date, set aside at least thirty minutes a day—more, if you can—to devote to scheduling your events.

Fifteen-minute marketing: Create lists—of cities and towns where you know people who will come to a reading, of possible venues, of writers you can team with, etc. Spending just a few minutes a day putting these lists together will let them simmer in your brain and spark new combinations and possibilities— and, after a few list-making sessions, you'll have the beginnings of your book tour ready to go.

Everyday marketing: As you go about your everyday life, open your eyes to the possibilities for promoting your events—look for bulletin boards (at local businesses, cafés, community centers, etc.) where you can post flyers; seek out local newspapers and magazines you may not normally read (for sending press releases). Keep an eye out for places that might distribute your postcards or bookmarks.

Also, during any moment of downtime, picture yourself at one of your events. Imagine what section of your book you might read; imagine the questions you'll get; envision a workshop you might offer. Think of new and different places for events, as well as the myriad types of events you could try. Let your imagination wander— you'll find all sorts of possibilities arising from these daydreaming moments.

A VIRTUAL BOOK TOUR

Virtual book tours are wonderful, especially if you're not able to do an extensive in-person tour. What is a "virtual book tour," exactly? It's simply another way to get out there and do what authors do—talk about your book, connect with readers, answer questions—only this way, you're doing it all virtually (on blogs, in interviews, and in virtual book club or classroom visits) instead of in person. The nice thing about this is that, unlike with a live book tour, on a virtual tour you can wear yoga pants the whole time. A virtual book tour is perfect for authors who aren't able to travel—and it's also a great way to supplement an in-person tour.

In terms of planning, however, a virtual tour may take as much work as a regular book tour; even if you're not traveling, there's a lot of scheduling involved. Below are a few examples of virtual events you can include on your virtual tour.

Throw a virtual book launch party.

You can host it yourself, or ask your publisher or a friend to host it. A virtual launch party is one that takes place on a blog instead of at a place. Pick a date, send out e-mail invitations, and show up online.

Be sure to set a time frame as well, keeping in mind that a virtual book launch party works well if it's a day-long event, so that people can drop in whenever they're available (before or after work, during lunch hour, in the evening, etc.). And of course, you don't have to sit there waiting for comments the whole time, but do check in as often as you can, at least every hour or so, and be available to "chat" about your book (i.e., to answer questions through the comments section).

To get the party started, introduce yourself (or have your blog host introduce you), and say a few things about your book, the publication process, the party itself—tell a story. Enlist a few friends to get the conversation going with questions or comments. Choose a few passages from your book to post throughout the event, which gives it the feel of a reading and also offers a chance for people to enjoy your book and to comment. Offer a giveaway—choose a random winner from everyone who came to the party, and send this reader a signed copy of your book.

Set a festive mood by posting pictures of food, cocktails, and images that depict the setting of your book, as well as other photos that add details and visuals. And, throughout the duration of the party, post on Facebook and Twitter that the party is going on, and invite people to join you for the next "reading," to stop by to be entered in the giveaway, and to join the conversation by posting comments.

Be a guest blogger.

Being a guest on writer/reader blogs is a great way to expand your audience. By now you will already have a blog, of course, and will have networked with other bloggers—so to plan your virtual book tour, approach those whose audiences are likely to be interested in your book. Then offer to do a guest post (see below for some content ideas). Aim to plan these posts on or around the book launch date (most important is that the book is available when the post goes live, so readers can buy it with one mouse click if they'd like), and always mention to your generous blog host that you'd love to return the favor someday.

In terms of content for guest blogs, be reader friendly. Talk about your book as well as your writing process. Offer things readers (and other writers) can use, such as top ten lists or a series of writing or revision tips. Talk about your writing routine or any special research you did for your book. Tell readers how you chose the name of your main character, or what music you listened to as you wrote. Just as you would at a live reading, delve into the process (and the person) behind the book, while offering glimpses of your writing. The idea is to introduce readers to your book while giving them a behind-the-scenes look as well.

And, finally, always include a bio, a book cover image, an author photo, a link to your website, and links to where people can purchase your book. Be ready to provide all this info so that the blogger who is hosting you doesn't have to scramble around to find it.

Schedule interviews and/or Q&As.

You'll approach bloggers the same way as you would for a guest blog, only instead of a guest post you can offer to do a Q&A or interview about the book, your writing process, or whatever best fits that audience. Be prepared to offer a review copy to the blogger, and have a few questions ready to suggest (things you want to talk about), which the blogger can use if he/she wishes and then add additional questions. You should also have a complete Q&A prepared for busy bloggers who prefer having a post that's ready to go.

Offer book giveaways.

You can offer giveaways on your own blog and other blogs, and of course, don't forget about Goodreads. Book giveaways are welcomed by most bloggers, as they draw in readers, and bloggers will usually ask you to send the book to the winner (so be sure to specify how far you're willing to send it, i.e., whether your giveaway is going to be limited to the U.S. or whether you're willing to mail it internationally). It's a great idea to order a box of extra books so that you can offer to do a giveaway with each guest post; also, many book blogs that offer giveaways also do reviews, so always ask if you can send a review copy along.

Offer an excerpt of your book.

You'll have an excerpt on your own website already, and always offer to send the link along whenever you do a guest post or an interview. For the excerpt on your own website, I'd recommend the first ten to twenty pages of your book—but for guest posts, you might submit shorter excerpts, such as a favorite scene (as long as readers will understand it out of context).

Look for opportunities to do taped readings, interviews, and/or podcasts.

There are a great many Internet radio programs, and online literary venues often accept audio submissions or do podcasts (visit Late Night Library, Blog Talk Radio, and Lively Words, as a few examples).

Getting scheduled on a local NPR station or other talk radio programs can be challenging without a publicist who has these media contacts—but it's not impossible, especially if you are a local author and/or your book deals in some way with community issues. Seek out potential venues and send a pitch letter; ask your publisher to send a proposal for programs that don't accept them directly from authors. Put together a press kit that includes a press release; an author bio; a Q&A for prospective interviewers; a fact sheet with interesting facts about some aspect of your book, whether fiction or nonfiction;

a page with blurbs and reviews; and anything else that might help a producer choose your book for an upcoming program. Make sure your proposal is as unique as possible, offer a sense of the person behind the book, and let people know what you hope readers will gain from it.

Finally, the nice thing about a virtual tour is that the possibilities are seemingly endless—you can go anywhere. The fact that you can do this also makes it a bit overwhelming. A few things to keep in mind...

Just because you *can* do everything doesn't mean you *must* do everything...

... at least not all at once. Launching a book into the world is a big deal, and it's tempting to want to do every single thing you can. However, you'll probably go a little insane if you try this. I suggest a virtual schedule that includes daily events the first week, then tapering it down a bit to two or three events per week over the following weeks. This will give you good buzz in the beginning, then allow you to breathe again. And remember that while book promotion is most important in the first few months, promoting your book is a long-term endeavor. Always keep an eye out for new opportunities to share your book with the world, months and years into the future.

Start developing relationships early.

You don't want to be rushing to get events lined up at the last minute, and you also don't want to be demanding of your fellow bloggers. Ideally, you already have a good network in place—if not, start networking well before your pub date. And, most important of all, ask not only what your fellow writers can do for you but what you can do for them: Offer them guest spots on your own blog; ask them how you can help them out, too.

Have FUN!

Don't make book promotion a chore, or you'll grow to hate it. Doing a great deal of writing and talking in a short period of time can get exhausting, so you'll have to find your own balance to avoid burning out. And while many people will tell you that you have to base all your events around the book launch date, I'm more of the mindset that "every week is book-launch week" in that, for one, book promotion never really ends; and two, it's not the end of the world if you don't fit it all into one week, or even one month. Rather than attempt to cram everything into a short period of time, you'll be better off in the long run if you think about ways to promote your book all year, and all the time.

See Kathryn Trueblood's Q&A on page 152 for more on virtual blog tours.

Everyday Marketing Tips

Fifteen-minute marketing: Anytime you have an extra fifteen minutes, seek out book blogs and make a note of which ones might be good for you to target with a review copy, interview, and/or guest article. There are hundreds and hundreds—and the more you explore, the better prepared you'll be to set up your virtual book tour.

Everyday marketing: Always be thinking of articles and ideas for possible guest-article proposals—you'll want to offer something relevant to your book as well as unique in its own way. Jot down ideas for top ten lists, for example, or take photos that will add interesting visuals. Having a file of possibilities on hand will allow you to hit the ground running rather than try to come up with a dozen different guest-post ideas on the spot.

BOOK CLUBS

Book clubs are not only fun as a reader, they are a writer's dear friend. Having your book chosen by a book club creates wonderful word of mouth that often keeps building. The question is: How do you get your book chosen for a book club?

First, let everyone you know that you've published a book and are willing to join their club for a meeting if they choose your book. You can show up in person as a guest, or you can join by conference call, Skype, or FaceTime. Book club members love having authors join their meetings, so be as accessible as you can (keeping in mind that they'll likely want to talk about your book for at least a little while without you in the room, so plan on joining for only part of the meeting).

To keep finding additional book clubs outside your circle of family and friends, post your availability on your website, as well as on Facebook, Twitter, and other social networks. Write a list of about ten discussion questions and post this on your blog and website as well; this will help show the ways in which your book is worthy of discussion. You might also host a giveaway, offering a signed copy to a book club host who chooses your book.

See the Q&A with Janna Cawrse Esarey on page 165 for more on book clubs.

CONSIDER A BOOK TRAILER

Creating a book trailer is a project you should embark upon only if you know it can be entertaining, enlightening, and a good tool for marketing your book. While book trailers can be a lot of fun, they can also be expensive and time-consuming, and there's not much evidence that they sell books. So consider a trailer if you have a fabulous idea, a budget, and/or the skills to do it well. It may not be worth the investment otherwise. For the right idea, it's fun and can help draw attention to the book—though keep in mind that a poorly done book trailer can actually hurt your book.

I debated whether or not to make a trailer for *Forgetting English* when it first came out in 2009. As a writer and reader, I must confess that I've always found the concept of a book trailer a little strange; while movie trailers for films are an obvious marketing strategy, I think it's a challenge for most writers (particularly fiction writers) to do justice to their books in a media that isn't an obvious match with the product, i.e., words and story and the imaginative collaboration they create with the reader. How to translate this into video was a mystery to me. Actually, it still is.

The main problem for fiction writers, I think, is how to portray our stories visually. We write because we love *words*, after all, and not all of us are also actors or have a great visual sense or have the budget to hire professionals. I've also found that attempts to dramatize a novel for the tiny screen can backfire in a huge way if not done just right. Many writers get around this challenge by focusing on something else other than the story itself, such as the author or the book's backstory—a great solution in that it gives readers a little something more than what they already know from the book's cover copy or author bio.

Challenges aside, there are definitely a lot of great book trailers out there. One of my all-time favorites is Dennis Cass's award-winning trailer, "Book Launch 2.0" (you'll find it easily if you do a Google search)—it's not only hilarious, but it does everything a book trailer needs to do: engage, entertain, and pique interest in the author and the book.

I watched dozens of book trailers after *Forgetting English* was published, and I saw a few good ones and more than a few bad ones. Worse, I came up with no great ideas for my own book. Promoting a short story collection from a small press has plenty of marketing challenges, and creating a book trailer seemed to be among the bigger ones.

So *Forgetting English* went trailer-less for nearly two years, and in the meantime my husband, John Yunker, published a novel, *The Tourist Trail*, and he, too, began to wonder if he should do a trailer. We began thinking of ideas, all of them terrible; we couldn't find a way to create a trailer for either of our books that didn't feel melodramatic or lame.

Then John had an idea—one that had nothing to do with the subject, content, characters, or themes of either of our books. But it didn't need to. And best of all, his idea incorporated both of our books. So we put together a script, picked up John's iPhone, and did the whole thing over a long weekend. It cost us nothing but time, and many readers (and especially fellow writers) got a kick out of it. The trailer told the story of married authors who grow obsessed with their sales rankings, and it was picked up and shared by *Poets & Writers*, Shelf Awareness, GalleyCat, and *The Seattle Times*, as well as many generous bloggers and Facebook and Twitter friends. If you want to check it out, do a Google search for "Love in the Time of Amazon.com."

As much as people enjoyed the trailer, however, it resulted in no more than a small uptick in book sales. Yet because we didn't spend any money, and because we had so much fun doing it, that didn't matter—and this is how I'd recommend you approach the making of your own book trailer. It should be fun and affordable, and book sales should be a welcome plus but not necessarily something you need or expect.

A few tips if you're considering a book trailer...

Remember the medium.

This is obvious, but important; as writers, we deal with words—now you'll need to deal not only with words but how these words are spoken; you'll need to deal with visuals and audio. It all has to come together to create just the right effect.

Keep it short and sweet.

Most book trailers are about two minutes long; don't go too much longer, or you'll risk losing your viewers.

Budget carefully.

I haven't found any solid evidence that book trailers actually lead to book sales (again, ours hasn't done a whole lot for our book sales, though thousands of people have seen it), so keep this in mind when you plan and budget. Professionally produced book trailers can get very expensive, so be aware of the costs involved and know that it might not be a great investment, especially since no one really knows how well book trailers actually sell books.

Think outside the book.

Consider ideas other than attempting to relay the story of your book in visual format, like taping an author interview, for example, or a book club meeting—something that offers a glimpse into you and/or your book while also being engaging to viewers. Also keep in mind that humor works well for book trailers.

Promote like mad.

Once you have a book trailer, the next challenge is to find ways to get people to view your book trailer; you can't just put it on YouTube and hope viewers flock to it. Promote it on your social networks, your website, your blog, and submit it to other bloggers you think might enjoy it.

Everyday Marketing Tips

Thirty-minute marketing: Jot down a list of your favorite moments in your book, whether these are whole scenes, descriptions, or a few lines of dialogue. Once you have a good list (aim for at least ten to twenty items), consider how any of these might translate to video. Would any of the scenes, played out, create an accurate reflection of your novel? Do you have any still photos that you might pair with a reading of a passage that you like? Would a scene of dialogue work in a trailer without being overly dramatic or seeming too out of context? Is there any royalty-free music that might make a good fit for some of these scenes? You may not come up with the perfect idea for a trailer based on this exercise, but it's a way to begin—and just take your time. Often, the best options will come to you after you've let ideas simmer for a while.

More thirty-minute marketing: As you think about your book in visual terms, think of still photos in addition to video. Check out visually oriented social networks like Tumblr and Pinterest, and work on creating a list of visuals that relate to your book. If your book is a historical novel set in Italy, for example, you might consider old photos or famous works of art; if you've written a cookbook, you'll list possibilities relating to food. Once you have a list of images, seek them out, whether from your own photo albums or others' (keep in mind that you'll need permission from the source for any photo you post that isn't your own). You might be inspired to take your own photos, or to pick up a pencil or paintbrush if you're artistically inclined. As one example, after *Forgetting English* was published I went through my own photo albums to find images of the places in certain stories, and then I shared them on Facebook with a little bit about the story (for "Translation Memory," for example, I posted a photo of the Japanese temple that is a major part of the story). There are many ways to be visual without doing video.

Everyday marketing: Keep your eye out for images in everyday life that relate to your book in some way, and have a camera or smartphone handy to capture it in a photo or short video that you can post on social media sites or your blog.

And, whenever you have spare time, check out other authors' book trailers to figure out what you like, what you don't like, and why. You might also find it helpful to read the books whose trailers you've seen—how accurately do the trailers reflect the books? Which trailers are most effective in drawing you in as a reader, and which ones leave you cold?

LOOKING AHEAD

As you look ahead to your approaching release date, think of other ways you can prepare for additional promotion opportunities. Below are a few tips and ideas.

Consider the holidays.

Determine whether your book is a good fit for any upcoming holidays, from Valentine's Day to Mother's Day to Halloween. Consider guest blogs, giveaways, op-ed pieces, and other ways to get your name and book title out there on whatever occasions may fit.

Look for speaking gigs.

Are there any organizations that might welcome you as a speaker, either in person or virtually, from travel blogs to support groups to your PTA? Again, think outside the bookstore and consider all options: local clubs, organizations, schools, and colleges. Having written a book, you are an expert in what you've done—writing, revising, research, and myriad other things—and you have a lot to share.

Think philanthropically.

If there's an organization you're passionate about that is in some way related to the topic of your book, team up with that organization for mutual benefit. For example, if your book has environmental themes, seek out environmental organizations where you might host an event; donate a book for a raffle, or donate a portion of your book sales from the day of the event. Keep in mind, of course, that raising awareness for the organization is as much the goal (if not more) as raising awareness about your book; be sure you give something back rather than simply use the organization as a way to sell books.

Keep up with current events.

Think about your book's topic and its relevance to what's going on in the world; even if your book is fiction, there may be an opportunity for you to submit op-eds, essays, articles, blog posts, and more to local and national media outlets. Stay on top of all the news, and prepare to write, submit, link, etc.—this is particularly important once your book becomes available. And it goes without saying, of course, that you'll want to connect your work to current events in ways that are respectful and truly relevant; don't ever risk taking advantage of a situation or making a connection so tenuous that you only hurt your book's image.

Check out specific media and issues.

If your book is set in Hawaii, look at Hawaiian media, travel magazines, in-flight magazines, etc., for promotion opportunities. If you've written a novel or memoir that deals with a certain issue, find organizations, support groups, and other ways to connect, as appropriate—again, this should be more about reaching out than about promoting your book; what you give will come back in the end.

Help reporters out.

Look into HARO (Help A Reporter Out, www.helpareporter. com) to see if it might be a good fit for you. This is a site that connects reporters with sources, so if you've written a nonfiction book, you're probably an expert that someone will eventually seek out for questions for a news story or web article. Even if you're a fiction writer, you may have some special knowledge gained from your research—and even if not, you'll often find reporters seeking input from authors on various aspects of writing and publishing. Keep in mind that sometimes reporters are looking for feedback on such random subjects as "men with hairy backs" or "women with psoriasis," so a lot of the information may not be relevant to you, and it can be time-consuming to go through all the requests for info. Also, be sure to check out the source before you take the time to respond to make sure it's a good fit and worth your while (sometimes the "reporter" is a start-up website looking for free content, which may or may not be helpful to you in the end). But it's a fascinating resource and well worth a try. Even if 90 percent of the time you don't find anything that fits, when you do, it can lead to good book buzz.

Everyday Marketing Tips

Twenty-minute marketing: Go through your calendar and make a note of any holidays you can connect to your book. Then, set up reminders for yourself to take advantage of whatever opportunities you have. For example, monthly magazines have a six-month lead time, so if you plan to submit an article or query for a Valentine's Day story, set up a reminder for yourself six to eight months before February. If you plan to pitch a guest post for a blog, find out what the lead time is and plan accordingly (some bloggers can post new material at a week's notice; others require stories months in advance). If you'd like to do a book giveaway, remind yourself about a month ahead of time so you'll have time to promote it.

Everyday marketing: Always keep your book in mind when it comes to your regularly scheduled life; opportunities for connection are everywhere, from your kids' school to your local college alumni program. Again, you want not to be mercenary but to establish meaningful connections that will lead to new relationships.

Part 3:
Book Launch and Beyond

If you've been able to do the planning outlined in this book so far, you'll be in excellent shape when you reach Book Launch Time. Being well prepared means your book launch is a fun and exciting time rather than stressful and overwhelming.

Even if you're not as well prepared as you'd like to be, always keep in mind that book promotion is forever—what you can't do in the next few months, you can do in the next few years. Many authors see their books as children, and it's not a bad analogy—just as your child is still your child when she goes off to college, your book is still your book after the launch period. It may not require quite as much time and attention, but you still want the best for it and will keep working toward that end.

Just Before Book Launch Time

CREATE A PRESS KIT

If you're working with a publisher, your publicist will have created a press kit—ask for all these materials and make them available on your website. If you're on your own, you'll need to create your own; if you're with a very small press, you may work on this in tandem with your publisher.

A good media kit should include:

- a press release that includes the book title, author name, ISBN, release date, publisher name and URL, a summary about the book, and author/publicist contact information
- an author bio
- an author photo
- an image of the book cover
- a Q&A with the author
- early reviews and/or blurbs
- contact info (phone, e-mail) for author and publicist

ARM YOURSELF WITH BOOKS

You'll receive a certain number of books gratis as part of your publishing contract; always order extras with your author discount. (Even better, see if you can buy some Advance Review Copies, or ARCs, before your launch date.) It's great to have extras to send to book bloggers and reviewers, to send to booksellers and anyone else who might host you for an event, and to offer to book clubs. If possible, ask your publisher for electronic ARCs (in PDF or other e-book formats); if you're self-publishing, create one yourself. Having electronic review copies available can save time, money, and trees.

At Book Launch Time

A FEW SMALL BUT IMPORTANT DETAILS...

Make sure your e-mail signature has a link to your website (which will, of course, have a link to where readers can buy your book, right?!).

Prepare an e-mail announcement to send to your subscribers.

Send save-the-date invitations out for your first events.

Be active on your blog and on social media.

CREATE YOUR AMAZON AUTHOR CENTRAL PAGE

On Author Central, you can add photos, links to your blog and website, video if you have it—and you can also list your events here. This is an excellent and important place to promote your book to a national readership. As an example, here's my Amazon author page:

www.amazon.com/author/midgeraymond

Keep your page up-to-date by adding event photos and linking it to your blog and Twitter feed (which updates your page automatically).

SPONSOR GIVEAWAYS

Goodreads and LibraryThing offer giveaways by authors. You should also host a giveaway or two on your own blog, at events, and as part of a virtual book tour. Keep in mind that while these aren't sales, you're reaching out to find engaged readers who will then talk up your book, choose it for a book club, or buy it as a gift for another reader—and this is invaluable.

EMBARK ON YOUR IN-PERSON BOOK TOUR

You've spent months making all your book-tour plans—now the fun begins. This next section provides tips and advice for how best to enjoy the events you've been anticipating for so long.

How to give a great reading

Reading to an audience is something you learn how to do well over time, through experience and mistakes. One of the most surprising things for me, when I first began doing readings for *Forgetting English*, was that I found myself wishing I'd read each and every story aloud one more time before seeing it into print—because once I began reading these stories aloud, I realized that I'd have changed certain words here and there so that they'd flow as well off the tongue as they seemed to on the page. So this leads to my first of many tips for having a successful reading...

Think ahead—way ahead.

When you're in the process of publication, think ahead to how your work will sound when you read it aloud, and make the changes you need to make. That way, when you're ready to plan what to read, you'll know that it will sound good, and all you'll need to do is practice. Which brings me to my next tip...

Practice.

You may think you know your work inside and out, but reading is so different from writing. And you'll also need to choose *what* to read, often from several hundred pages (see below for how to choose). Practice reading your selection aloud as many times as you need to. Read for a few people to get feedback on your pacing, emphasis, and delivery. Some writers use audio or video to gauge how they're doing—also a great way to practice. And if you live in a city that offers open-mic events, go to them and participate as often as you can. The very best way to get comfortable in front of an audience is to practice in front of an audience.

As part of the preparation for our joint book tour, Wendy Call and I visited Seattle's Jack Straw Productions, the Northwest's only non-profit multidisciplinary audio arts center, to record excerpts from our books. It was there that I received the following wonderful tips from producer Moe Provencher as I stumbled through a practice reading.

- Mark up the text from which you're reading so that you'll know when to pause, what to emphasize, etc.

- Develop a facial expression that reflects a character's voice and/or mood; when you use your face to express something, this mood and tone will come through in your voice.

- Read far more slowly than you think you need to— to the point at which you feel ridiculous—and this will likely be the perfect pace.

- Breathe.

When choosing what to read, less is more.

When *Forgetting English* first came out and I was doing a lot of readings, I experimented with what to read and for how long. Once, I read an entire story (about forty minutes of reading); other times, I would read for ten minutes from one story; and still other times, I would read from three different stories for five minutes each. When Wendy and I did our joint book tour, we often bookended our events with readings—brief readings in the beginning and at the end, with the majority of the event being workshop, discussion, and Q&A.

Aim to read a passage that doesn't require a lot of explanation— for example, read the first few pages of your first chapter. If you want to read something from the middle of your book, make sure you offer enough context so that your reading makes sense to your audience, and again, only do this if you can explain the backstory in a few words.

Another thing to keep in mind is that you should feel free to edit what you're planning to read. Once for a reading, I edited a short story down by about 30 percent, reading the shortened version in its entirety. I did this to stay within the time limit I was given, but I also found that it made for a smoother reading, as I was able to take out some of the dialogue (always a challenge for me to read aloud) and to omit some of the subplots, which quickened the pace of the main narrative. And don't feel as though you need to read from your printed book; it can be much easier to print out pages in large type and read from those.

Sometimes the best way to learn what works is to give different things a try—and, having done that, I can definitely recommend reading less and chatting with readers more. My forty-minute reading was, fortunately, well received (if you do read for that long, be sure you do it in front of a friendly crowd who'll happily sit through it and not throw things at you; also, give them a heads-up about the duration of the reading so they won't get restless)—but I've done a long reading only that one time, and I doubt I'll ever read for that long again. For one, it's easier to read shorter passages; two, you don't risk tiring an audience; and three, it makes available more time to chat about the book and to take questions. Remember that readers are there to get a taste of the book, but just a taste—they're also there to get what they can't get from the book itself: a glimpse of who you are as a writer. You'll want to read enough to give readers a feel for what's to come, but the idea is that they'll be buying the book, so you'll want to offer something they can't take home with them.

Support the venue.

If you're reading in an indie bookstore, support it with a purchase, whether it's a book or a box of greeting cards or a bar of Theo Chocolate. If you're in a library, ask if you can donate a copy of your book for their collection. Always find a way to give back.

Offer something extra to readers.

Bring bookmarks or postcards, buttons or pens—any little something to offer guests at your event. It's nice to offer little extras as thanks for supporting your event—and if they don't purchase the book but leave with a bookmark, they'll be reminded of it and might be inspired to buy it later.

Bring *everything* you might need.

From water to reading glasses to tissues to cough drops, bring whatever you could possibly need. Keep a list of things, just in case. It's amazing what you forget ... I've read without water (challenging) and without reading glasses (doubly challenging), and I once forgot to bring a copy of my own book, so I had to borrow one from the bookstore (embarrassing). There is no such thing as being too well prepared.

Be comfy.

Wear comfortable shoes; you'll likely be standing for a long time. Find an outfit that is comfortable (so that you're not sweating or freezing) and also makes you feel confident and awesome. As mentioned above, be comfortable visually as well—print out the passage you'll be reading in nice, big type if your book's type size is too small or if you find reading glasses cumbersome (or if you tend to forget them).

Bring extra books.

Even when I'm reading at a bookstore that already has copies of my book, I always bring five to ten extra copies along, just in case—it's far better to lug them along than to lose these extra sales and readers. Bookstores sometimes under-order, and having been at bookstores that have sold out and needed my copies, I'm always glad to have them available. Granted, my book is slender and in paperback, so this is easy ... but even if your book is a hardcover, it's a good idea to have at least a couple of extras. If you do find yourself in a situation in which you leave readers without books, get their e-mails and follow up yourself, offering to send a signed copy.

Keep developing that mailing list.

Pass around a sign-up sheet or a guest book at every event for anyone who wants to know where you'll be next or to hear about your next project.

Be ready for anything.

I keep my events low-key on purpose—no PowerPoint, nothing even remotely high-tech—so I never worry about the inevitable broken projector or other possible malfunctions. But if you do need to bring or use equipment other than yourself and your book, always have fallback solutions, just in case.

Talk to readers.

Don't simply read but *engage*. Open your reading by thanking everyone for being there; say something nice about the city you're visiting. Tell them what you're about to read, why you chose it. Then, after your reading, invite questions. If no one asks anything at first (don't worry—they all have questions; they're just shy), simply jump right in yourself by saying, "One question I get a lot is … " and answer it. This will open up the conversation. As one example, you can talk about what inspired your book or certain scenes. It's always fun to learn what's behind the scenes of an interesting book, and by doing this, you offer readers more than what's between the pages.

Sign books.

When it comes to signing books, every writer has a style of his or her own. Even if you're brand-new to book signing, you've probably had many authors sign their books for you; take a few moments to study the inscriptions and to think about how you might sign your own books, the idea being to extend warmth and gratitude to your readers. Remember that you'll sign books on the title page, and you may notice that some authors cross out their printed names when they sign books, apparently a tradition whereby the author is replacing the printed name with his or her signature. You might add the date and the name of the bookstore, conference, or book fair, and anything else you can to make the inscription as personal as possible. And always ask the reader to spell his or her name, just in case.

Get photos.

If you have a friend or family member in attendance, give this person the role of photographer. If you're solo, bring a camera to hand over to your event host. Let people know you're taking photos to use for publicity, just in case anyone wants to get out of the frame. And then, be sure to use these photos—post them on Facebook and on your website, and send them to your publisher and/or publicist. Images are key if you hope to get a little media attention, so always aim to get a few photos at every event.

Remember that size doesn't matter.

One of the biggest wake-up calls for a new author is showing up to a reading that is poorly attended. (This is why the promotion covered in Part 2 is so very important—prepare well, promote your events like crazy, and you may not have to worry about this.) Yet, inevitably, most authors have an event that isn't as well attended as they'd like—and that's okay. Give the same engaging, lively reading whether there are two people in attendance or two hundred; make each reader feel welcome and important. Even if only one person shows up to hear what you have to say, connect with that reader.

And keep in mind that the smaller turnouts can be intimate and fun in a completely different way than a standing-room-only crowd (which is also fun, of course). With a very small group, you have the opportunity to engage on a different level, to get to know your readers and allow them to get to know you—and if this goes well, the word of mouth this brings can be even better than a larger reading that wasn't as personal.

In the end, the most important thing is that you have fun—this is something that readers will remember—and often the most fun and surprising events go well beyond the book itself.

Everyday Marketing Tips

Thirty-minute marketing: Take thirty minutes to follow up after each event—you may need less than half an hour, but do allow yourself enough time for these important tasks. First, always thank the people at the venue that hosted you—send an e-mail at the very least, but keep in mind a handwritten note is always the warmest way to go. Also, post photos from the event on your website, blog, and/or social networks. Send personal notes/e-mails to friends and family who showed up with other friends in tow, as well as anyone who provided extra support in any way. Show your gratitude in abundance.

Everyday marketing: Spend moments of downtime thinking about your upcoming events in a positive way. Just as an athlete is coached to imagine executing a perfect pitch or a perfect dive, envision the same for yourself: an enthusiastic crowd, a confident reading, a successful event. Picture each event exactly as you want it to be, and keep this positive energy within you as you go about your book tour.

Embark on your virtual book tour

Many of the guidelines for good in-person readings apply here as well, more or less—support your host, through social media; offer something to readers, such as a giveaway or a discount for signed copies; engage with readers. Most important, however, for embarking on your virtual book tour, is to have the plans outlined in Part 2 ready to execute—the further in advance, the better.

For example, if you pitched a guest article for a blog four months before your book launch date, write up that blog post (a rough draft, at the very least) soon after making the proposal, so that during the flurry of book-release activity, you won't have to scramble to put together the post. For one, you'll be short on time, but even more important, you want to submit a good article to your host. Sending a hastily written, sloppy post to someone who has generously offered you space on his or her blog is not only disrespectful but it will reflect poorly on you and your book. So be sure that you have gotten a good head start on the materials you'll need to submit for your virtual tour.

Also, remember that you'll need to be as present for these virtual events as you would be for an in-person event. If you're doing an online launch party, make sure you check in at least once an hour, if not more, to be available to readers. If you're doing a radio interview over the phone, get dressed up even if no one will see you; you're likely to sound more professional and engaged if you're in regular clothes than if you're still wearing pajamas. (And see the Q&A with Elizabeth Austen on page 184 for more tips on how to prepare for and give great radio interviews.)

Finally, be sure you have plenty of books on hand for the giveaways you're planning to do. Make a list of the blogs and social networks on which you've offered giveaways, and be sure you budget as well as order enough copies in advance. Sometimes a book blogger who reviews your book will offer her own copy for a giveaway, but often she'll ask for another one, then send you the name of the winner, and you'll mail the signed copy. Don't forget to let bloggers know if you're unable to mail books overseas (which can get very expensive).

HANDLING REVIEWS: THE GOOD, THE BAD, THE NONEXISTENT

When *Forgetting English* was first published by Eastern Washington University Press in 2009, I learned—after the fact and much to my dismay—that it had never been sent out for reviews. It wasn't long before I also learned that my publisher would close within the year, which answered the question of why—but I still had to deal with the fact that I had a short story collection to promote without a single review.

And that was a little depressing.

Authors (rightly) expect their publishers to send out review copies (if there's ever any doubt, ask), but of course this doesn't guarantee that their books will actually *be* reviewed. With some 200,000+ books being published in the U.S. annually, it's a challenge, particularly for new and emerging authors, to get reviewed by the major media outlets that can get your book the attention you want and need. So what can an author do to help create some publication buzz when the reviews aren't coming in?

Among the best advice I got from authors when *Forgetting English* was published was to use my author copies for promotion purposes. I'd been planning to give them all away—what could be more fun than to shower friends and family with free books?—but then I realized that my fellow authors had very good reasons behind their advice.

First, if anyone's going to buy your book with great joy and pride, it'll be your friends and family—so let them. It doesn't cost them all that much, and it'll support their indie bookstores or your Amazon ranking, and that's all good.

Second, you'll need to send complimentary copies to those who were instrumental in the writing or publishing process, from those who helped you with research to those who offered blurbs; anyone who donated time and energy to you without asking anything in return certainly deserves a signed copy of your book.

And, finally, whatever copies you have left are best used to help promote it—given today's challenges, from the economy to dwindling attention spans, we authors need all the help we can get.

And, whether you've gotten big media reviews or not, you'll still want to take advantage of the myriad options for generating buzz and/or keeping it going. So here are a few tips for getting reviews (or additional reviews) and making the most of them...

Check out book review blogs.

About six months before your book comes out, research book review blogs to see which ones might be a good fit for your book as well as receptive to reviewing it. You'll want to approach bloggers who have a good number of followers (these are your potential readers) as well as comments (which shows that the reviews are being read and responded to). Also be sure the bloggers read and review in your genre and that the reviews are of the quality and sensibility you hope for in a review. It's best to query first so that you don't send a copy that may end up in the recycling bin; if a blogger is interested, he or she will get back to you. Because publishers often offer advance copies to book bloggers as well as more traditional media, check your list against the review list of your publisher so that you don't duplicate efforts.

Be your own publicist.

If for any reason your book doesn't get sent out for reviews, don't give up—simply send copies out yourself. You won't get anywhere with such industry media as *Publishers Weekly*, which require copies months in advance, but your local newspaper will probably pay attention, and may even do a feature article along with a review, especially if you have a local event planned. Target any publication you think would be receptive and a good fit. Alumni magazines and newsletters are a great resource, as are literary magazines, especially if they've published your work in the past.

Think outside the box.

Don't limit yourself to traditional book review sections of publications but also look at other possibilities, from travel columns to cooking editions. Target radio stations, university publications, community newsletters—any venue or publication that might offer a good audience for your book and/or topic.

Remember that every day is book promotion day.

Don't give up on getting reviews even well past your publication date. When *Forgetting English* was reissued by Press 53 a year after it went out of print, I reached out to new bloggers and even did another book tour—all of which led to many new readers, even though the book by then was two years old. Always keep an eye out for publications that might be a good fit, or for a local news story that you may be able to contribute to. There's never any reason to stop promoting your book; there will always be someone out there for whom it's brand-new.

Ask your fans to go public.

If readers tell you how much they love your book, ask them to review it on sites such as Amazon, Goodreads, LibraryThing, and Barnes & Noble. Having good reader reviews on these sites will get the attention of online shoppers, and though it feels awkward to ask, you'll get over this once you see a few nice reviews up there. You don't have to beg or plead; simply tell people who already like your book how much a nice review will help get the word out and how much you'd appreciate it.

Remember how subjective the process of reviewing is.

If you do happen to get a bad review, try to remember that it's not personal. All book reviewers are human beings with personal tastes that may not align with what you've written or how you've written it. Recognize that no writer or book can satisfy every reader, and, because the book is out there and there's nothing you can do to change it anyway, do your best to ignore anything negative. And don't attempt to respond to bad reviews, even if you feel the reviewer was sloppy or missed the whole point of the book; this approach never goes anywhere good. Just let it go.

And keep in mind that, in the end, while reviews are wonderful and helpful, they won't necessarily make or break your book. Many bestsellers have been made by word of mouth alone, so always remember what *you* can do for your book, focusing on what is in your power to accomplish rather than what's not.

Everyday Marketing Tips

Fifteen-minute marketing: When a new favorable review comes out, be sure to set aside enough time to post it on your website (create a page for reviews if you don't yet have one). Also, share it on your social media networks, always being sure to include thanks and a link to the review, whether it's a blog or the *New York Times*.

Everyday marketing: Again, don't neglect to ask for a public review (on Goodreads, Amazon, Barnes & Noble, etc.) when someone tells you how wonderful your book is—most people don't think about this and don't know how important it is for you and your book. And if someone with a blog compliments your book, offer a guest post, interview, or Q&A, if appropriate.

Beyond the Book Launch

In this digital age, books can live forever—and for their books to live well, authors are wise to keep promotional opportunities in mind well after the launch date (many bestselling books were in print for years before they became bestsellers).

So, moving forward, you'll need to balance your book promotion with your regularly scheduled life as well as with the new writing you're doing. Establish a daily routine that may be less rigorous than the months leading up to your book launch and just beyond but that nonetheless keeps your book out there and keeps your mind open to new opportunities.

Here are a few examples of what you can do in ten minutes a day, in thirty minutes, and so on. Assess your schedule and figure out how much time you have on each day of the week to devote to book marketing.

First, be sure you have a Google alert set up for yourself and your book title, so you won't miss any news or press about your book. Also, subscribe to RSS feeds for topics that are related to your book's themes for news, blog posts, etc.

If you have ten minutes a day...

Log on to Twitter, post a few tweets, and retweet anything

you find interesting and/or relevant to your work.

Around the holidays, remind people that a signed copy of a book makes a wonderful gift!

Remind people that your book makes an excellent book club pick; post your discussion questions to Facebook or Twitter, or e-mail a few friends with the questions and let them know you can join a future meeting. Offering a free signed copy to the host is generous and fun.

Give thanks to someone who's helped you—whether it was a writer who gave you advice or a reader who gave you a five-star review. Consider thanking this person publicly on social media, if appropriate; this can be a great way to show appreciation as well as lead new readers to your work (note: this works only if it's someone who will enjoy the public display of gratitude!).

Take ten minutes to do something nice for a fellow author, such as tweeting an upcoming event or writing up a Goodreads review. Generosity is a beautiful thing, and it always comes back to you.

If you have thirty minutes a day ...

Log on to Facebook; post an update, photo, or link that is relevant to your book; engage with a few friends; and share anything you find interesting.

Find a fellow writer and offer to do a Q&A trade in which you interview each other about your books, then post the interviews on your respective blogs. This gives you both some great blog content as well as a little extra exposure.

If you have an hour a day ...

Write several short blog posts and save them as drafts so that you'll have your next few posts ready to go. Aim to get a new blog post up on your blog at least once a week.

Keeping the holidays in mind, look ahead and find the next holiday that is relevant to your book—it could be anything from Thanksgiving to Groundhog Day—and set up an event, write a blog post, or plan a book giveaway.

Stay on top of all the news, and if there is anything happening that is relevant to the topics and/or themes of your book, take the opportunity to write an op-ed or a guest blog; at the very least, include links on your social media networks. It goes without saying, of course, that you'll want to connect your work to current events in ways that are respectful and truly relevant.

If you have two hours a day ...

Think of articles you can write for magazines, newspapers, and digital media that relate to your book in some way (whether you've written nonfiction or a novel). Find specialty publications that might publish a Q&A based on the expertise you've gained in writing and researching your book. You can also use this special knowledge to give talks and lectures as well as write and submit articles.

If you have half a day ...

Visit your favorite organizations (either locally or online) to see what is new with their fundraising efforts—and offer copies of your book. Books make great auction items, especially if they're part of a larger package (if your book is set in Italy, for example, it would make a nice addition to a European travel package at a charity auction). You could also put together gift baskets around the theme of your book (if your book is about living a green life, for example, a basket might include your book, some organic teas, vegan chocolates, etc.). Other fun auction items include naming a character in a forthcoming book or story after the highest bidder, or offering a writing workshop or a book club event.

If you have a whole day ...

Take a trip to a nearby city. Contact local bookstores and/or libraries in advance to see if they might be interested in an event.

DON'T GIVE UP

Most important to remember when it comes to book promotion is not to give up—ideally, not ever. After all, you never know when your book might take off, but if you stop talking about it, it probably won't go far. The Q&A with international bestselling author Jenna Blum on page 242 offers inspiration as well as why it's so important not to give up on your book.

ONWARD!

As you'll see from Jenna Blum's Q&A on page 242, it's never too late for your book to find its readership—the only thing that matters is that it does, whether it's six months after its initial publication, or four years. Yet many writers, often due to the limitations of their publishers, treat book marketing as a 100-meter race instead of what it really is: a marathon. Or, for most of us, an ultra-marathon.

And what this means is that you'll need to pace yourself. The months before and after publication will be a flurry of activity, but keep in mind that you'll need to endure beyond these chaotic months—so avoid burnout. Know that you can't fit in everything right now—but that you'll be able to fit it in later. Recognize that some things (like industry and media reviews) usually do need to happen before or just after book publication, but that opportunities will still exist much later—with book bloggers, for example. And remind yourself that for book clubs and all readers, every book is new if they haven't yet read it; it doesn't matter whether it was published a month or a year ago.

This is what this book is designed to help you achieve: continued promotion of your work, while living your regularly scheduled life—and discovering an audience for your work that keeps growing over time.

Part 4:
Q&As with Authors and Experts

Authors

AUTHOR KIM WRIGHT

Kim Wright has been writing about travel, food, and wine for more than twenty-five years and is a two-time recipient of the Lowell Thomas Award for Travel Writing. She is the author of *Love in Mid Air* and the *City of Mystery* series. She lives in Charlotte, North Carolina.

What are the biggest differences between promoting a book published by a big publisher versus promoting a self-published book?

At the time that my novel *Love in Mid Air* came out in 2010, I had a reasonable amount of support from my publicity team at Grand Central. Especially the online publicist, who helped to arrange a blog tour that was quite successful.

But things have changed significantly at the Big Five houses since then. Budgets are shrinking and heads are rolling and any staff left is criminally overworked. What I understand from my friends who've more recently gone with a Big Five house is that you just can't count on getting anything in terms of publicity, especially if you're a midlist or new writer. That's one thing that's always been a bit mystifying about the big houses. They spend the majority of their promotional efforts on authors who are already established—'cause yeah,

Nicholas Sparks and Jodi Picoult really need those ads—and debut writers struggle along on their own.

Of course, the one advantage the Big Five can still give their authors is distribution to bookstores, so if you go with a big house you might have readings, signings, a launch party, etc. There might be efforts made to get you reviewed in newspapers and magazines. But the key word in both of those sentences is "might" because, once again, these things don't happen as much as they used to. I don't know anyone who's done a book tour during the last two years, no matter how they've published.

So ... bottom line, there's not as big a difference as there used to be. Most of the promotional work falls to the writer whether you've gone Big Five, small press, or self-pub.

How is marketing fiction different from marketing nonfiction?

The biggest difference is that it's easier to zero in on the target reader and market for nonfiction. For example, each year for thirty years I've updated my travel guide for Fodor's, titled *Walt Disney World With Kids*. Based on the title alone, it's not hard to figure out who's going to buy this book. You're either going to Disney World or you're not. You either have kids or you don't. And a lot of nonfiction is like that. It's very easy to target a book precisely to its intended market and very easy to build an author platform.

Fiction is trickier. Look at the title of *Love in Mid Air*— what the heck does that mean? Or the first book in my self-published mystery series, *City of Darkness*. The titles are evocative but vague. You need explanation before you could guess who would want to buy the book.

So I think fiction requires a little more finesse to market. You have to explain the book in a way that pulls people in and convinces them that even though they don't need to read this book, they might want to.

What is the single most successful thing you've done to promote your books?

With the mystery series I've just started, the most successful thing, without question, has been putting the book in the Amazon KDP Select program. This means that it is available to be borrowed by Amazon Prime members and also that it qualifies for free promotions five days out of every ninety. Both of those perks are huge because they boost you into the Amazon algorithms, and your book starts to be recommended to Amazon customers. For online sales at Amazon, it is all about the recommendation queues, bestseller lists, and being recognized as being a mover and shaker in your genre. The more you show you have a readership—through your sales, reviews, and longevity on the lists—the more they will promote you.

Of course, that's what's working right now. When *Love in Mid Air* came out in 2010, blog tours were the rage. My online publicist helped me to arrange a tour in which the book was featured on seven blogs a day for ten days in a row, and that got the book a ton of attention and helped establish immediate buzz. But it seems blog tours are fading, and now it's all about free online promotions. In 2014, it will undoubtedly be something else. The biggest thing I would tell writers is to be willing to learn and grow and change in terms of book promotion because this is an industry that's changing fast. What worked for your best friend might not work for you. Heck, what worked for you in April might not work for you in November.

What aspect of book promotion has surprised you the most?

The willingness of other writers to help. There's a real fraternity among the recently published. Through social media, I've reached out to quite a circle of fellow authors. And we're very quick to give each other advice and feedback, help each other find writing or teaching gigs, fill panels, whatever. You would think it might be competitive or there might be some passive-aggressive digs, but I have to say I've found extraordinary kindness. Nobody really understands what you're going through except another writer.

What have been your biggest marketing challenges? How are these challenges different based on fiction versus nonfiction, and big publisher versus small press versus self-publishing?

The single biggest challenge facing all writers, whether they write fiction or nonfiction, whether they're conventionally published or self-published, is precisely the same: finding a readership.

It used to be that the question facing writers was "Can I get published?" People were obsessed with finding an agent, then praying that the agent could sell the book. It was a narrow gate. Not a lot of people got through it, but those who did could expect that once they were on the other side they could get significant help from their editors, agents, and publishers.

Now that's no longer the question. With the advent of self-publishing and the fact that most readers are shopping online for books and the whole e-book explosion ... it's a different world. I always say the good news is that anybody can get published. And the bad news is that anybody can get published. Because there are so many books in the marketplace—more than six times as many now published per year as there were two years ago. And there certainly aren't six times as many readers.

So the question is not "Can I get published?" but "Once I get published, what do I need to do to help my book succeed?" The challenge is standing out in an oversaturated market, and I think that's a matter of knowing who your target readers are, where and how they shop for books, and tailoring your strategies to make it easy for them to discover your books.

What advice do you have to offer new authors?
Begin building your promotional network long before you think it's necessary. I used Facebook, Twitter, and the blogs to connect with other writers, but you also can use these methods to create a dialogue with potential readers. It takes time to build up your list of Twitter followers or Facebook friends, and if you want to be reviewed or featured on blogs you need to start making those overtures months before your book debuts.

Writers wait too late. They're so concerned with writing and editing the book that they wait until it's about to come out to think, "Gee, I may need to start thinking about marketing." The most intense marketing push is indeed the first six months after a book comes out, but you need to start laying the groundwork long before that.

POET SUSAN RICH

Photo credit: Rosanne Olson

Susan Rich is the author of four collections of poetry, *The Cartographer's Tongue: Poems of the World; Cures Include Travel; The Alchemist's Kitchen*; and the forthcoming *Cloud Pharmacy*. Her poems have been published in the *Antioch Review, Alaska Quarterly Review, Poetry International,* and *The Southern Review,* among others, and her fellowships include an Artist Trust Fellowship from Washington State and a Fulbright Fellowship in South Africa.

Tell us about how your books came into the world.

All four of my books are published by Dennis Maloney, the creative force behind White Pine Press. I am very happy to have a twelve-year relationship with my publisher. From what I know, it's a rare thing in the poetry world.

I first contacted Dennis on behalf of South African poet Ingrid de Kok to see if he would like to publish her work in the United States. At the same time, Dennis noticed an article I'd published in *Poets & Writers* about de Kok's work. The irony is that Dennis published my work and not Ingrid's. Five years after *The Cartographer's Tongue: Poems of the World* came out, I was lucky enough to meet Dennis in person. (Prior to this meeting, all of our correspondence was over e-mail.)

When I asked Dennis why he chose to publish my book, he said simply that I was the only poet who had ever contacted him on behalf of another poet, and that fact had caused him to take a serious look at my work. I've told this story to many young poets struggling to see their work in print. The message I hope they come away with is: Everything we do for others also supports our own writing lives—often in ways we could never anticipate.

What are the most successful things you've done to promote your books?

I learned this from a poet friend, and it's very simple: "Ask for what you want." Be clear on what makes an event or a project a positive experience for you. When one festival in Vermont invited me to read, I wrote back to say I'd love to come but I needed accommodation for my stay. At first the organizer said that he couldn't accommodate me, but a few weeks later he came through with rooms offered to the festival by a lovely hotel. Since then I have asked museums to host events for free and hotels to give over their penthouse for a performance. There is no shame associated with asking for what you want—and this works especially well when working with other writers.

Here's one example. For my book *The Alchemist's Kitchen*, I decided that I wanted to set up a national tour. This goal sounded overly grandiose to my ears and to my budget (poets are not sent on tours by their publishers), but it was what I wanted: a new challenge. Over a two-week period, I visited

San Diego, Boston, and Miami for events in each place. In each city I had friends to see, so I knew it would be fun no matter what else happened. In each city I read with other writers and made contacts that led to other projects. Going on the road facilitated new contacts and new places to do book promotion—because I asked.

What aspect of book promotion has surprised you the most?

I'm always surprised that book promotion is actually fun. I am an introvert at heart—happiest with my own company. The idea of "selling" myself makes me want to run off to another planet. However, after several books I've found that when a book comes out, I look for other "new" authors in the same position so we can help each other. The writers I've met are overwhelmingly a generous lot. We share creative promotional ideas and our favorite bookstores to read in. This goes a long way toward casting the whole expedition as more of an adventure than a burden. My newest idea, "borrowed" from Colleen Michaels, a poet in Salem, Massachusetts, is to create an "Improbable Places Poetry Tour." Colleen and her students at Montserrat College stage poetry readings where you least expect to find them: a flower shop, a Laundromat, a store window, and a bank. I'm working on an event right now that takes place in a hotel penthouse.

As an author and busy professor, where do you fit book promotion into your schedule, and how vital do you think it is to devote time to this aspect of being a writer?

It has to be fun. I look for a chance to bring friends together and to challenge myself to try a new approach to a necessary task. When it is no longer fun, I won't do it.

What advice do you have to offer new authors?

About six months before *The Alchemist's Kitchen* was published, I looked at my computer screen and knew that I had to start promoting my book. There was dread in my heart as I came to this realization. I had already been through the book promotion process twice before with my other two collections. That night, out of quiet desperation, I came up with one simple idea. Why not e-mail women I knew who had books coming out or who I believed were book savvy? What would happen if we pooled our energies and supported one another by sharing promotional ideas? I had no idea if others would want to work together, but I decided to ask.

I e-mailed ten women, and that same night the majority e-mailed me back saying that they indeed wanted to join forces. One woman suggested two friends she had that also might want to join. Three years later, we are a vibrant group of women writers from poets to fiction writers, photographers to memoir writers. We've put on events together and promoted one another's work on our blogs and in our communities. Each month we challenge one another to pay "literary dues" by doing one thing to promote one of the other members' work. We also laugh a lot and share stories of our time on the road. Our first point of business was to come up with a name, and we voted on "Book Lift" with the sense that we would help each other lift up our books and carry them into the world.

Each time we meet for happy hour, I come away with one new idea to pursue and the knowledge that I'm not alone. It makes all the difference.

AUTHOR SHARAN NEWMAN

Sharan Newman is a medieval historian and author. She received her master's degree in medieval literature at Michigan State University and her doctorate at the University of California at Santa Barbara. She is the author of more than a dozen fiction and nonfiction books, including *The Real History of the End of the World*, *The Real History Behind the Da Vinci Code*, and the Catherine LeVendeur mysteries.

Tell us about how your first book came into the world.
I was about twenty-three years old and decided to write an Irish-like fantasy because I had done an academic paper on Irish history and had lots of research left over. This was long before personal computers. I spent a couple of years writing it and then sent it out to several publishers. An editor responded. I rewrote the book, and it came out in 1976. It was remaindered almost immediately, but it gave me a foot in the door.

What have been your most successful promotional opportunities?
Genre conventions are great. I've been to mystery, science fiction, fantasy, romance, and historical novel conventions,

and they are a wonderful way to let people know about my work and meet me.

What aspect of book promotion surprised you the most?
That, even with a good publicist, most of the work is up to the author. Bookstore signings were a shock. At the beginning, I was put at a table at Waldenbooks with people asking me the way to the bathroom and no one buying books. It's sort of a trial by fire. I learned that the best thing for me is to have a talk advertised. Then people will show up even if they don't get the book. But I really don't want to have to sign at the chains again, and soon there may be none left.

How has book promotion changed over the years you've been writing and publishing your work?
It's a new world. The Internet has made it possible to promote even if your publisher has no budget for you. It also means that one can spend more time promoting than writing. I don't balance it very well, and I don't do enough of either, I fear. I have a website, my own blog, a group blog of mystery writers, and am on some LISTSERVs and on Facebook. I'm told I have to learn to tweet.

What has been your biggest marketing challenge?
Getting bookstores to put my books where people can find them. There's not much one can do about this, but, again, good Internet promotion can overcome the problem. So far, Facebook is the best connector. My website is also good for background information on the books, what I've been doing, speaking engagements, etc. I don't know about the blogs. I don't seem to say anything viral.

What have you found are some of the biggest differences between promoting fiction versus nonfiction?

Nonfiction is easier because there is a niche topic to discuss. I get a lot more TV and radio interviews with the nonfiction. But you can create a topic from the theme of your book even if you write fiction. Talking about the topic is better than just telling the world how great the book is.

What advice do you have to offer new authors?

Don't give up. Learn what you can. Go to conferences and conventions. Buy drinks for established authors, and they'll give you lots of good advice.

One thing about promotion is that you can't be pushy. Value yourself and your work, but respect the people you are trying to sell to. I've seen too many authors destroy their careers by being rude or self-important. And—one thing I'm bad at— have some written, paper material to give people. Also, it's sad but true: Word of mouth is still the best way to sell books, but it's up to the author to get the word started.

$\backsim$

Spent $20k

AUTHOR WENDY CALL

Photo credit: Kathy Cowell

Wendy Call is a writer, editor, translator, and teacher of creative writing. Her narrative nonfiction book, *No Word for Welcome,* won Grub Street's 2011 National Book Prize for Nonfiction and the 2012 International Book Award for Best History/Political Book. She is co-editor, with Mark Kramer, of *Telling True Stories,* and her nonfiction, translations (from Spanish) of poetry and fiction, and photography have appeared in more than fifty magazines and literary journals.

Tell us about how your book came into the world.

My book began as a series of twenty essays and narrative nonfiction pieces that I wrote while living and working in southern Mexico. I had received a two-year fellowship from the Institute of Current World Affairs, and they published my writing. I returned to the U.S. in the summer of 2002 and began to put together a book proposal, to seek an agent, and to learn the deep difference between a collection of five-thousand-word narratives and a single ninety-thousand-word book—as well as the difference between *writing* a book and *publishing* a book.

On the publishing side: I approached nearly fifty agents before I found two—in the same month, after nearly five years of sending queries—who were interested in representing my book. I chose the agent who had more experience selling narrative nonfiction. She circulated the proposal (and later, the full manuscript) for about a year, and was on the verge of giving up when the University of Nebraska Press tentatively offered me a contract. The contract, contingent on a significant revision, included no advance. Because of the peer review process (common at university presses), a year elapsed between my agent sending UNP the proposal and the press sending me a contract.

What was the single most successful thing you did to promote your book?
It's hard to judge the most successful thing, but I did the most important thing long before I decided to write a book. Before I moved to Mexico, and began the writing project that would become *No Word for Welcome*, I devoted nearly a decade to full-time work as a grassroots organizer. What I learned as an organizer—how to solicit help from others, how to work with the media, and how to keep seeking a *yes* in spite of many *no*s—all helped me enormously with book promotion.

Just as a campaign organizer would, the first thing I did was create a budget: $20,000. (Since I had no advance, that amount was completely self-financed.) I organized six months of full-time travel and promotion, squeezing in enough teaching and writing work to earn that full amount during the same timeframe. That is to say, every penny I earned during those six months went into promoting *No Word for Welcome*. That might sound like an enormous budget, but it was actually quite lean. I decided to travel coast to coast, flying from my home in Seattle to Boston, and then driving back. I set up my cross-country itinerary based primarily on where I had friends and colleagues who would house and feed me. A few even helped me contact local bookstores, put up flyers, and sent e-mails to their friends.

I also secured three months' work that included housing. I spent two months in New England, doing events while I worked as a writer in residence at a lovely national park in Vermont. I stopped for another month in Iowa, teaching an intensive creative writing class at Cornell College while I completed events in seven different states. During my entire tour, I only had to pay for hotel rooms for two nights, when I was driving the 1,500 miles between events in Lincoln, Nebraska, and Yakima, Washington. I traveled with coolers of food, a hot pot, and picnic supplies, to cut down on restaurant meals. Less than half of my total budget was devoted to those six months on the road.

My publisher printed a limited number of advance review copies of *No Word for Welcome*. I wanted to promote the book more widely, so I devoted more than $2,000 of my budget to printing and mailing additional review copies. More than half of those extra copies were sent out by the publicist I hired to secure radio interviews. He did an excellent job, landing me thirty-five radio interviews all over the country. Many were with small, local stations, but I completed several interviews with statewide NPR affiliates and two with nationally syndicated programs: the PRI / BBC show "The World" and "Viewpoints." Even some of the local interviews, like one on the KPFK Morning Show in Los Angeles, led to attention far from LA, because the podcast posted to the web was publicized on several blogs.

My publicist's work was limited to radio exposure. My publisher and I did the rest. UNP landed three book reviews for me: *Midwest Book Review, Publishers Weekly,* and *Orion* magazine. Meanwhile, I queried two dozen reviewers who had written about books similar to mine, asking if they were interested in review copies. About ten replied that they were; one wrote a review. More effective was writing to friends and colleagues who had a professional interest in the book's subject and asking them if they might consider doing a review. That led to several nice reviews, including a prominent literary journal and a large trade association magazine—two very different audiences for my book.

Organizing events also required many review copies. Many of the bookstores and colleges I contacted to ask about possible readings needed one or more review copies to make their decision. My publisher sent some of those copies, but it was much more efficient if I mailed them myself. I also sought event "co-sponsors" for events—nonprofit organizations that loaned their name to the event and promoted it to their local membership. Those organizations needed review copies as well.

My six-month tour included more than fifty readings and other events—the result of more than one hundred pitches and *lots* of follow-up communication. I shared some of this work (and the fun of the events) with other writers. My Seattle book launch was a joint event with a friend whose novel was published the same month. And Midge Raymond and I collaborated on ten events in six states—taking advantage of similar themes in her short-story collection and my book.

My events were evenly divided among traditional bookstore

readings, events at conferences and colleges, and readings in nontraditional venues. That latter category included a Oaxacan restaurant (my book takes place in Oaxaca, Mexico), a labor union hall where I had organized meetings fifteen years earlier, the library at the college I attended more than two decades earlier, the visitor center of the Vermont park where I served as writer in residence, and my favorite Seattle bar. Sometimes I had to bring my own books, but in several cases, a local bookstore or organization handled sales.

Bookstore event managers have told me that stores generally expect a 20 percent sell-through rate—meaning that one of every five people attending the event buys the book. My rate for both bookstores and nontraditional venues precisely hit that target. I found conferences, book festivals, and colleges led to a far lower rate: only about 2.5% in my case. That said, I reached a much broader audience at those latter venues, which was important to me. I wrote my book out of personal and political conviction, so I welcomed every opportunity to talk about it, whether that resulted in book sales or not.

The audience size for my bookstore events averaged eighteen. Two events had only four people—including the bookstore staff! Still, I appreciated every person who made the effort to come hear an author about whom they knew nothing. As I learned from Karen Allman, the brilliant events manager at Seattle's Elliott Bay Book Company, a crucial audience at bookstore events is the staff—and the real benefit comes long after the event date. The most successful in-store events, Karen explained to me, are those at which a bookseller is captivated by your book and later recommends it to customers. Of the eighteen stores where I had events, this happened twice. Thanks to the enthusiasm of independent booksellers in Lincoln, Nebraska, and Portland, Maine, I've sold more books in those two cities—where I know almost no one—than in the two (much larger) cities where I've spent most of my adult life: Seattle and Boston.

What aspect of book promotion surprised you the most?
As naïve as it sounds, the sheer *quantity* of work shocked me. I began working on promotion part-time six months before my publication date, and full-time about three months in advance, and that was not soon enough. Other than my hometown Elliott Bay Book Company, the first six bookstores I approached turned me down. Even those "No, thanks…" replies came only after many, many hours of figuring out whom to contact, crafting personal query letters, sending review copies, seeking a local co-sponsor, answering detailed questions, or trying (over and over) to get the right person on the phone.

What was your biggest marketing challenge?
For me, the single most difficult task was requesting testimonial blurbs for my book cover. Of all the moments in the decade between idea and book when I had to gather my courage, the hardest of all was asking famous authors to take the time to read my book and consider blurbing it. Fifteen months before my publication date, I wrote to a dozen writers I admired, with whom I had the slimmest connections, and asked them this enormous favor. I am forever grateful to the six authors who agreed to read my book and put their names behind it.

What advice do you have to offer new authors?
This is no time to be shy. Nor humble. Put yourself out there; push yourself a bit past your comfort zone. When this seems impossible, ask an extroverted friend to coach you. (I have a quote from Sandra Cisneros—who is deeply generous as well as brilliant—on the cover of *No Word for Welcome* only

because a fearless friend talked me through composing the e-mail to her and then pressing "send.")

Make sure to let everyone you have ever met, and have an e-mail address for, know about your new book. I found that I couldn't predict with any accuracy which friends and colleagues would be interested in *No Word for Welcome* and happy to lend a hand in its promotion.

Devote as much time and money as you can possibly afford—but *only* what you can afford—to promotion. Set priorities, but try a variety of strategies. For example, I devoted $500 of my budget to submitting my book for awards. My publisher offered book copies for six award submissions. I wanted to submit to a dozen different awards, so I bought the book copies for the other six awards, and I paid all the submission fees. It seemed like a strange way to spend five hundred bucks, but it was worth it. I won two awards, bringing a bit of renewed media attention to *No Word for Welcome* nearly a year after its publication date. (One award came with a $1,000 check, so you might say I doubled my investment.) Even if I'd not won either award, the submission process put my book in front of movers and shakers in the literary world.

What might you do differently, given what you learned from your book tour?

It was quite a challenge to secure bookstore readings for a book about a little-known region of Mexico, published by a university press. I was lucky to have the chance to read at bookstores in a dozen states, including independents I have long admired, like San Francisco's Booksmith, Milwaukee's Boswell Books, Iowa City's Prairie Lights, and of course Elliott Bay Book Company. Still, I devoted a huge amount of time trying, and failing, to secure bookstore events in several other cities, including Boston, Los Angeles, and New York. Looking back, I wish I had devoted more time to alternative venues from the beginning.

As happy as I am to have a hardcover original of my first single-authored book, next time, I'll be content with a paper original. Selling a hardcover that retails for nearly thirty bucks is an enormous (and soon-to-be anachronistic, I think) challenge.

What were some of the best aspects of your book tour?
I've focused on the hard facts and cold reality here, but I want to emphasize what a great adventure I had on my book tour. It was a real privilege to travel to so many places and talk about a subject that had absorbed much of my life for a dozen years. My fifty tour events took place in eighteen states between Maine and California, as well as in two Mexican towns that are featured in the book. I am deeply grateful to each one of the 1,600 people who took time out of their lives to come and hear stories about a part of Mexico that was utterly unknown to most of them. I'm even more grateful to the fifty bookstores, organizations, colleges, and festivals that hosted me.

In the end, it wasn't at all a lucrative venture, but it was a deeply satisfying one. When I first began writing the narrative that would become *No Word for Welcome*, while living alone in rural Mexico, the biggest lesson I learned was: *Everything must be its own reward.* I realized that even if my writing never became a book, what I learned along the way would be gift enough. The same maxim applies to book promotion. It's hard to connect specific strategies to numbers of books sold. Nonetheless, I enjoyed every event that I did (even for an audience of four) and everything *was* its own reward.

Author Kathryn Trueblood

Kathryn Trueblood's most recent novel is *The Baby Lottery*, a Book Sense Pick in 2007. Other awards include the Goldenberg Prize for Fiction, judged by Jane Smiley, and the Red Hen Press Short Story Award. Her stories and articles have been published in *Poets & Writers, The Bellevue Literary Review, The Los Angeles Review, The Seattle Review, Glimmer Train,* and *Zyzzyva,* among others. She is an associate professor of English at Western Washington University.

How do you get ready for a blog tour?

The first thing you want to do is find the constellation or neighborhood you belong to on the Internet. This is a form of market research. In the words of the great poet Robert Frost in "The Road Not Taken," "way leads on to way," and nowhere is that more true than the Internet. So if it means you start at Powells.com or Amazon.com looking for titles similar to yours or writers you especially like, that's fine. The next step is visiting the websites of these other titles and authors. I'd also advise going to the *New York Times* archive and putting in your subject + blogs because the top blogs often get written up.

What you're looking for is what I call "a matrix blog"—in

other words, a site that links to a large collection of blogs. When my book came out in 2007, Joan Blades, the co-founder of MoveOn.org, was publicizing a book and documentary film titled *The Motherhood Manifesto* that became the catalyst for a political movement called MomsRising.org, which is dedicated to lobbying for the rights of working women and families on Capitol Hill. Since I believed my novel, *The Baby Lottery*, would appeal to politically conscious working women, this was an ideal matrix site. It contained a huge list of blogs I could link to from the site. This was what I needed to get going.

After that, I got obsessed. As far as I can tell, that's what research on the Internet means: getting obsessed! I spent some very absorbing hours visiting the blogs and websites listed on the MomsRising.org page, and from those blogs, I found other blogrolls, and I could also see which blogs came up repeatedly, i.e., had high visibility. I started making lists, and I found that tiered lists were helpful: my first choices, my second choices, etc.

Another thing you'll want to be sure you have on your website is a downloadable press kit. This means that any blog writer reviewing your book or interviewing you has immediate access to the publicity materials they might need—they don't have to e-mail and request them, and you don't have to e-mail back and send them. My downloadable press kit included a press release, a background to the book article, an author's bio in several lengths (long, short, and shortest), and most importantly, PDF files for my book cover plus an author photo. Having a downloadable press kit on your website shows that you're professional and ready to go. Blog writers were able to grab what they needed, and it meant that my book cover appeared every time someone reviewed the book on their blog, sometimes even the cover for my first book as well.

What are some of the pros and cons of a blog tour versus an in-person book tour?

I see them in complementary roles. As a writer, I like belonging to my region, so I make an effort to read locally. Since newspapers, and by that I mean the local weeklies as well as the big dailies, won't review a book unless it's tied to an event, you have a much better chance of getting a review if you are appearing somewhere locally. *The Seattle Times*, the *Seattle Post-Intelligencer*, and *The Stranger* reviewed *The Baby Lottery*, which gave me some nice meaty quotes to put into my web release, and this in turn gave me some credibility with bloggers. Because you have a much shorter time frame with an in-person book tour, I focused on that first. But so much had changed since my first book was published in 1998, I had to employ different tactics. When *The Sperm Donor's Daughter* came out in 1998, I put together 250 media kits myself, and then couch-surfed from Bellingham to Los Angeles, garnering reviews and radio spots as I went along.

With *The Baby Lottery*, I asked my publisher to give me 80–100 bound galleys for publicity. This is something you have to ask for early in the game, and since your publisher may not ask you how many galleys you want, you need to be prepared to negotiate for this. Galleys are the cheap, uncorrected proofs of your book, but they're bound and often bear the actual cover, and sending them out is much cheaper than sending the real thing, even with your author discount. My strategy with my second book tour was to go where large concentrations of readers already gathered—conferences and book festivals. My genre happens to be literary fiction, but I think a writer of any genre could adopt this strategy with a little research.

It turned out my publisher was willing to give away a box of books so that I could attend the Pacific Northwest Booksellers

Association conference in the spring, where I was one of many featured authors at dessert reception. Giving away fifty books meant that I met fifty booksellers in one night, and I am sure that helped *The Baby Lottery* become a 2007 Book Sense Pick, which meant it appeared on the website of every independent bookstore nationwide for the month of July. After that, I went on booking myself and made appearances at Wordstock in Portland, Get Lit! in Spokane, and the Montana Festival of the Book in Missoula. My book was published in June, and by November, I was finished with my in-person tour: six months total. I was ready to concentrate on blog touring.

The terrific thing about a blog tour is that it extends the life of your book dramatically.

To bloggers, as long as your book has been published in the last year, they still consider it newsworthy and review-worthy. So, I spent the next nine months blog touring while also teaching full time. Yes, I cancelled my social life, but I have durable friendships, fortunately, and I certainly never felt lonely. I worked on the blog tour on weekends and at night, and it was such a great pleasure to converse with these really smart people who wanted to talk about the issues in my book, because they were also dealing with the tensions of raising children while having careers or creative lives. They were incredibly candid and engaging people.

I started by approaching the online magazines first and was thrilled when I broke through: *The Feminist Review*, *Mamazine*, and *Literary Mama* all gave favorable reviews to *The Baby Lottery*. *Literary Mama* asked me to write an essay for their blog about parenting and writing, which I did; "Motherhood and Writing" is still up on their site.

At the time, online publicists were just starting up, and the freelance ones promised ten sites for $1,000. When I saw that, I took it as my personal challenge to reach ten as my own publicist. And I made it! My book was reviewed by *Motherhood & Words*, *Mommy Writer*, *Viva La Feminista*, *Jumping Monkeys,* and the *Opinionated Parent*, among others. I was even invited to appear on Twit TV, a subscriber podcast network that went out to over 10,000 people. It turned out the *Jumping Monkeys* website, which is run by Megan Marrone, was also a show devoted to parenting issues. I sat down at my computer one afternoon, put on headphones, and felt as though I were right there in the studio with co-hosts Megan Marrone and Leo Laporte. That was one of many bright spots on the tour. I can't tell you how affirming it is to talk to people who find your book compelling and make connections from it to their own lives.

What is the best way for an author to approach a blogger who might be a good fit for a tour stop?
Send a short query letter, accompanied by your web release. Whether your book is fiction or nonfiction, you need to figure out the angle of social relevance that your book offers and articulate it. Why is this a topic that needs to be part of the cultural conversation or that enlarges a conversation already taking place? That's your pitch, and it belongs in your query letter. If the book serves a niche audience, you need to make a strong case about what your book offers that others do not.

What were some of the tangible results of your own blog tour, and how would you recommend authors manage their own expectations?
I know that my blog tour helped me sell books, but when I sat down to write *The Baby Lottery*, I did it because I was not finding books that authentically conveyed the lives of working

women; it's very much a chick-lit or romance environment. So for me to hear directly how deeply my book resonated with women was its own reward.

We live in a celebrity culture with a mass-market mentality, and yet we are the most diverse nation on earth. Why should mass-market expectations govern our ideas of success? If your book reaches an audience that values it deeply, is that not a measure of success, whether you have sold 2,000 copies or 200,000 copies? My favorite book on this subject is *So Many Books: Reading and Publishing in an Age of Abundance* by Gabriel Zaid. He says: "The true art of publishing involves placing the text in the middle of a conversation: knowing how to feed the flames."

What's the best way to get bloggers interested without a track record—i.e., how does a new author put together a successful web release?
Almost all the print magazines now have blogs, and they need constant content. You could be the next expert of the day, if you frame it right. Remember that you are offering them something they need.

You've got three options: see if they review books and make an inquiry; give them an excerpt from your book that they can run; or offer to write an article for them.

Here are the things you need to put in your web release.

Nonnegotiables:

- At the top: your book cover image.
- At the bottom: book title, name and contact info for your publisher, pub date, number of pages, ISBN, price, and the logo if you like.

- Prominently displayed: offer of a review copy, a booking date, or a live interview.

- Your e-mail and website address.

- At the bottom: your photo and a three-line bio (no more than that). If you don't have big credentials, then offer information that would make you seem like an interesting interviewee or that emphasizes why you are qualified, in your own way, to speak powerfully on your subject.

Below are some things you can pick and choose from.

Negotiables (for the body of the text):

- Excerpts from great reviews, especially a chunk that does a good job of letting the reader know what the book is about and why it is relevant to your target audience.

- Blurbs and testimonials. It's always best to have someone else say great things about your book.

- Your pitch—a paragraph or two in a journalistic voice, so that it can be easily adapted by the media.

- A self-contained chunk from your book, especially good for fiction or nonfiction. If it's a how-to book, a list of compelling topics covered.

- Relevant information about events, speaking engagements, or teaching related to your book.

- An arresting or engaging biographical fact that makes you uniquely situated to tell this story now.

Author L.J. Sellers

L.J. Sellers is an award-winning journalist and author of the bestselling Detective Jackson mystery/thriller series as well as standalone thrillers. A Readers' Favorite winner, L.J.'s novels have been praised by *Publishers Weekly*, *Mystery Scene*, and *Suspense Magazine*, and her Jackson books are the highest-rated crime fiction series on Amazon.

Tell us about how your first book came into the world, and how this led you onto the path of being (and remaining) an independent author.

I self-published my first Detective Jackson novel in 2007 after receiving rave rejections from major publishers. That was before the Kindle was released and print-on-demand publishing became available to individuals, so I spent a small fortune on a print run of 3,500 mass-market paperbacks. Then I worked like a madwoman to find a distributor and reach out to bookstores. I got lucky, and the novel was well received and reviewed. So I wrote two more books in the series, which were picked up and published by a small press. I spent ten times as much money promoting the books as I made in royalties. Despite the wonderful reviews from readers, I strongly considered giving up the series and even wondered if I should continue writing fiction. Then I was laid off my newspaper job, and the year 2010 looked very bleak for me.

But during those years, e-books had emerged as a growing market, and POD became a viable option for print books. So I started looking at my options and decided to upload my unpublished stand-alone thrillers to Kindle to see if I could generate some income. I quickly realized I needed to leave my publisher, get the rights back to my Jackson series, and self-publish every story I had—both as an e-book and as a POD print offering. Which I spent a good chunk of the year doing. After I uploaded the fourth Jackson novel in late October, I turned down freelance work for nearly a month and spent eight hours a day promoting my novels. I wrote blogs and articles, posted in forums, bought a few newsletter ads, and gave away hundreds of e-books on Goodreads and LibraryThing.

The results were astounding. By the end of the year, my series was a Kindle bestseller, and I was making a living selling e-books. Since then I've published another five books, and I'm living my dream of being a full-time novelist. But that term is a little misleading. Because I was self-published with ten books on the market, I spent as much time running my business as I did writing the next novel.

But all that has changed. Last year I signed an eleven-book contract with Amazon Publishing—nine backlist titles and two new novels. For the record, it's the only publisher I even considered selling to. Amazon's contracts are writer-friendly and generous compared to other publishers. And now that the new versions are on the market, Amazon is heavily promoting them, and my sales have doubled. I'm finally free to write full-time. My lifelong dream.

What was the single most successful thing you've done to promote your books?

My success came in two waves. The first big breakthrough happened when I ran an ad in the Kindle Nation newsletter. I sold hundreds of books in one day, and that boosted my Jackson series' sales enough to earn support from the Amazon algorithm, which in turn led my books to the top of Kindle's police procedural list. But the algorithm support doesn't last forever, and my sales eventually tapered off.

My second—and bigger—breakthrough came a year later when I enrolled my novels in Amazon's KDP Select program, then did a couple of Amazon-sponsored giveaways. That earned me wider exposure than I'd ever had before and broadened my readership substantially. All last year, my sales were healthy and steady without the support of Amazon's algorithm, and that was an exceptional experience.

What aspect of book promotion has surprised you the most?

In the summer of 2011, when my sales started to taper off, I bought several print ads in crime-fiction magazines and didn't see any effect at all. That was surprising and disappointing. The other unexpected thing was discovering how much I enjoy promotion. It's exciting and interactive in a way that writing isn't. I need to do both to stay happy and engaged.

What has been your biggest marketing challenge?

The biggest challenge in marketing is to keep finding new opportunities. Because what worked in 2010 quit working in 2011 when every other author started doing the same thing. And what worked six months ago is no longer as effective now. The market is constantly changing, and the competition is fierce. So I continuously have to find and try new marketing ideas, and it's time consuming.

Can you tell us how you're expanding into German and Spanish, including why you chose these languages and which others you may add in the future? How does the translation process work?

Now that I've signed with Amazon, it will produce foreign language versions. But right before I partnered with Amazon, I was fortunate that a small German publisher contacted me and offered a contract for my Jackson series. Because of the high cost of translation/production, they didn't offer an advance, but the royalty split offered was very fair. Right now, American fiction is popular in Germany, which is why Amazon is starting there with my books, so I encourage successful indie authors to query German publishers.

The other option is to find a translator and produce your own version. Before signing with Amazon, I had begun that process for a Spanish version of my series. I'd been thinking about it for a year; then Amazon opened a Spanish language store, and I knew it was time. Through networking—sending e-mails to everyone I know—I finally found a translator I could afford. She'd already completed half of my first Jackson story—*The Sex Club*—when I signed with Amazon and asked her to stop. I had also lined up a Spanish proofreader, and the combined services would have cost around $2,000. But the fact that Amazon is now producing a Spanish-language version of my work means that I was right to initiate that investment. The Spanish-language market is significant and will continue to grow, and I know several indie authors who have entered it with their own resources.

What advice do you have to offer authors who plan to self-publish?

The first thing is to have your work evaluated by objective professionals in the industry to determine if it has commercial potential. If your novel is marketable, then you have a green light to make the investment you need to be competitive. At that point, you need to decide what your goals are. Do you simply want to publish your book to see it in print for family and friends? Will fiction be a sideline, or do you want to make a living from it? Determining what you want out of the self-publishing experience will help you decide how much time and money to spend. Because if you want to sell well and earn a living, the next step is to invest real money in editing, cover design, professional formatting, and promotional spots. You also should commit to spending a couple hours a day on promotion—social networking, blogging, posting in forums, and querying book reviewers. If professionals don't consider your work to be marketable or you don't have the time and money to invest at an appropriate level, then you may need to accept that writing novels is a hobby and whatever you invest may never be recovered. That may sound harsh, but it's the reality of a very competitive market.

Can you tell us how e-books compare with print books in your experience? Which do you feel will be more important for independent authors going forward?

I sell 500 e-books for every print book, and I expect that ratio to grow as more readers buy tablets and other devices. For independent (unknown) authors, readers are much more likely to try a low-priced e-book than a $15 trade paperback, so e-books are vital to expanding your readership. Offering a print version is reader-friendly and requires very little additional investment, so I recommend it as well. But for me, and most of the indie authors I know, print versions make very little money compared to e-books.

What do you feel are among the toughest decisions independent authors face as they embark on the journey of self-publishing?
One of the biggest decisions indie authors face is whether to join Amazon's KDP Select program and be exclusive to that one retailer, or to upload and sell from as many retailers as possible. Some things to consider are:

- Amazon has 65% of the overall e-book market and represents 98% of indie author sales. Also, recent legal rulings about agency pricing mean that Amazon will likely gain even more market share.

- Other retailers often discount your books, leading Amazon to discount your books. When you lose money on 98% of your sales, it's significant.

- Most e-book retailers (Nook, Sony, Kobo, and Apple) heavily promote the books that Big Five publishers pay them to support (co-op for bestselling authors). Amazon is the only retailer that offers a level playing field with giveaway opportunities and algorithms that support indie books.

Author Janna Cawrse Esarey

Janna Cawrse Esarey is the author of *The Motion of the Ocean: 1 Small Boat, 2 Average Lovers & a Woman's Search for the Meaning of Wife* (Simon & Schuster). A *Publisher's Weekly* Summer Fave, *Today Show* rec, and *Parade* Pick, it's the true story of a woman who sails across the Pacific on her honeymoon, only to find her relationship heading for the rocks. Watch Janna's book trailer at www.byjanna.com.

Tell us about how your book came into the world. Were book clubs initially a big part of your marketing plan?

I was a high school English teacher who always dreamed of writing but never. Had. The time. When we set sail on our honeymoon (two years across the Pacific in a very small sailboat), I started working on a novel—of which I have 129 versions of the first paragraph. I quickly realized I had no idea how to write a novel and few resources aboard to learn. So I followed that old adage: Write what you know. Musings about love at sea turned into magazine submissions, turned into rejection letters, turned into magazine articles (and more rejection letters; those never stop), and eventually a nonfiction book proposal. It took pitching *The Motion of the Ocean* at several writing conferences before I found a fabulous agent (at William Morris Endeavor), who sold my idea to a fabulous editor (at Simon & Schuster), who gave me just seven months to write the whole thing. This seemed impossibly short, but the deadline was firm because it dovetailed with the due date of my second daughter.

So it was while nursing a newborn that I hatched my schemes for Finding My Audience, which is, I think, a better way to think about book promotion. I knew book clubs would be key for a couple reasons. First, I was in two book clubs myself, and I knew the kinds of books we most liked to discuss: those that give us perspective on life's big questions. Even while writing my book I was conscious of this, and it drove me to share more, bare more, and make myself (despite my temptations to gloss over or defend or explain every little thing) open to interpretation. My book would do the most good, I knew, when it made people think. And dream. And talk.

Which brings me to the second reason book clubs are so important: Book clubs *talk*. Rebecca Wells said she knew *Divine Secrets of the Ya-Ya Sisterhood* was going big when book clubs began attending her readings en masse. See, not only do book clubbers read voraciously themselves; they read and tell. Word of mouth is how books find their people.

How did you get your first book club gig, and what can a writer do to get on the radar of book clubs?
My very first gig was actually before *The Motion of the Ocean* came out. A local college class was assigned to create promotional materials for several new books, mine included. (Pays to have friends who teach!) These amazing students convinced the campus bookstore's book club to read ARCs (advance reader copies) and recorded the group's discussion. They also made a book trailer—a short video—to promote

my book. (I know, lucky! You might see if students in your area could do the same.)

My next gig, also pre-publication, was with Simon & Schuster's in-house book club—a huge honor—but it made me understand why my editor had gone to bat for photos, a map, and a book club kit in the back (discussion questions, activities, and an interview). We had to fight hard for all these extras. With no budget for a map, I drew it myself, and I also helped write the discussion questions since I knew I didn't want any dry, English-teachery reading comprehension questions. (Hint: Questions that make readers interpret the text or reflect on their own lives work best.) These extras—whether in traditional publishing or self-publishing—can be a lot of work, but they definitely attract book clubs.

To prepare for other book group gigs, I set up a section for readers on my website that included an expanded version of the book club kit as well as recipes, my personal backstory, and, of course, the book trailer. You could also include a blog, inspirational quotes, behind-the-scenes info, or photos of where you write. Visit your favorite authors' websites to get ideas. I also ran a promotion: Choose *MOTO* for your book group and receive one free, signed copy. My publisher gave me a box of books to give away in this manner—very effective!

Now, a website is a passive form of promotion—visitors arrive already having heard of your book. Expand your reach by including your website and another link or two (Amazon, Facebook, or Twitter) in your e-mail signature. Anyone who receives an e-mail from you will learn about your book and, through the social media links, your availability to book clubs.

Speaking of social media, Facebook is an author's best friend. Why? Because you can reach out to your number-one fans—

your friends! Set up both a personal Facebook profile and an author or book page. Here you can post author events, links related to your book topic, the inside scoop about writing and publishing, tidbits from your personal life, and, of course, photos and anecdotes from your book club chats. Connecting with one book club via Facebook—and posting about it—will often lead to connecting with another book club. You can also try a Facebook ad that will post only to your friends' friends, or friends of those who have already "liked" your book page. You can set your budget and your bid so it doesn't break the bank.

Twitter also provides a quick, easy way to mention upcoming book club chats, post group photos, or share possible discussion questions. Reflect afterwards with favorite quotes or questions from the evening. Use a hashtag (#bookclub) to get as many views as possible, and create a hashtag for your own book, too (#MOTO).

Other ways to help book club members find you online include joining—and being active in—communities such as Goodreads, She Writes, and Red Room. Use your blog to post anecdotes and photos from book clubs you meet. Mention your availability to book clubs in newsletters to readers. And, finally, offer review copies or guest posts to book review blogs or blogs related to your topic. This can be time intensive, but it's worthwhile for blogs that have a good following.

There are many ways to find book clubs offline, too. Visit your local bookstore and offer your availability to their in-store book clubs or groups they sell to. Some stores offer discounts to book clubs that routinely buy through them—and even place these book sets on a special "book club" shelf. Good advertising! Also get in touch with your local library and discuss book club options. You might donate a "book club kit": a handful of books, discussion questions, and your contact information in case they want to chat. Depending on your genre, you can also contact local reading groups through your bookstore or library (mystery book clubs, for example), and offer to join them. And, finally, reach out wherever you can—to your alumni association, civic club, faith center, fraternity/sorority, or other organizations related to you or your book topic.

Finally, any time you talk about your book, make book clubs part of your message. Mention your availability in your author bio and at events. Encourage reviewers to cite book club appeal on Amazon and Goodreads. Tell your hairdresser, your dentist, your barista, your cousin that you "love to talk to book clubs." I find those words much easier to say than anything about my book. And then, inevitably, one interested reader turns into many.

How should an author prepare for joining a book club discussion?

First, set it up. Choose the time, date, and format—phone, Skype, or in person. Will they call you or you call them? Provide backup numbers just in case. If it's an in-person visit, is it for dinner or just drinks? (The latter on an empty stomach could make for an interesting evening.) Discuss how long you'll participate and other expectations—will you be giving a talk, as in a literary salon? Will you be answering questions? Will you simply be joining in the conversation? It's best to give book club members thirty to sixty minutes to congregate before you join in.

You'll also need to do some prep of your own before showing up. If you're going to be there in person, be sure to map your location beforehand and leave yourself plenty of time to get there. I speak from experience that smartphone maps sometimes mislead! Bring contact info for both the person who invited you and the location host, just in case. If you're using Skype, test it beforehand.

If you're one of the many authors who is more articulate in writing than in person, think about likely questions and prepare answers. Also, come up with two or three questions to ask the group yourself. These do not have to be original; you may choose from the discussion questions in your book club kit since groups rarely answer those one by one with an author present. Or ask a final question that rounds out the evening and brings your book's central theme into focus. For example, since my book is about dreaming big, I always ask members what their own big, hairy, audacious goals are. They often learn something about each other they didn't know!

Before the gathering, show your enthusiasm by posting about the upcoming meeting on your Facebook page—you could even post on your host's Facebook page. Send an e-mail to the group telling them how excited you are; if you only have the host's e-mail, he or she can forward it. You might let them know what your format is (see below) or where your book is available. You might add Facebook links and invite them to post a group photo or their thoughts on your Facebook page. If you do a lot of book club meetings, you'll find it easiest to create a standard e-mail that you can personalize for each group. This way you'll be more likely to remember this step, as well as the very important thank-you note (see below).

Also, be sure to get permission to take and post photos—the most efficient way to do this is to mention you'll be posting the photos from the meeting on your website and/or social media; unless anyone objects, you have implied consent.

Once an author does get invited to join a book club, what is the best format for the meeting?

I start by asking group members to introduce themselves and share their deepest, darkest secret. Just kidding. But you might want to offer a prompt that relates to your book. After intros, the discussion starts. Since I'm not the host, I go with the flow, sometimes just listening to their conversation, but usually answering lots of questions. At the end I ask the group my own questions. And then, via phone or Skype, I thank them profusely and sign off. In person, you might offer to stay and chat, or you might excuse yourself so they can catch up socially. It helps to set expectations beforehand.

And as far as etiquette goes, here are a few more tips:

- Be honest and open. If you're a memoirist, remember it's your book's job to say things most people are afraid to say, so don't worry about them knowing your intimate details. But then it's okay to uphold personal boundaries face-to-face. Demurring with a light or humorous tone works best, e.g., "Oh, I'm too shy to answer that."

- Be positive. Don't bring up bad reviews. Don't complain. And don't get defensive of your work. Humor and humility are your allies.

- Remember: People have different tastes. Some may not have loved your book, but they can still like you. In fact, people will inevitably like your book more after having met you.

- Be gracious. Don't worry if some haven't read your book, and don't point out that the answer to their question is in the book!

- Don't drink too much—unless you're seeking

notoriety, which I don't recommend.

- Don't overstay your welcome, but on the other hand, don't race out too early. Again, set clear expectations beforehand.

- At the end, take a photo with the whole group holding your book, and offer to sign their books. Don't be disappointed if they all have library books; better to have readers than buyers!

After the meeting, document it via social media (as discussed earlier). And finally, send a gracious thank-you note. Again, you'll want to create a standard e-mail for this, but personalize it by mentioning the food, the surroundings, or something that happened. Include a link to their book club photo on your Facebook page or website. You might even ask for Goodreads or Amazon reviews if you can keep it light and humble. Also, add them to your database and let them know you'll keep in touch by sending them your author newsletter. Finally, ask book clubbers to recommend—or even pass on—your book to other readers. Remember, one more reader can turn into many as long as you inspire them to talk!

AUTHOR ZOHREH GHAHREMANI

Zohreh Ghahremani (Zoe) is an Iranian-American artist and writer. For twenty-five years she taught at Northwestern University Dental School, ran a dental practice in the Chicago area, and wrote. In 2000, she moved to San Diego and became a full-time writer. Her first novel, *Sky of Red Poppies*, was selected for KPBS's *One Book, One San Diego* in 2012. Visit her online at www.zoeghahremani.com.

Tell us about how your book came into the world.

I have carried the main story of *Sky of Red Poppies* around the world for years. It has been written and re-written multiple times, but the character of Shireen, my high school friend, has always been at its core. Selfless and modest as she was, I knew she would never tell her story, so I decided to become her voice. I also wrote this to offer my three American children a slice of life in my homeland of Iran, as I knew it. I wanted the novel to open a window for them to see a place and time that will never be again, and to better understand their parents' background and culture. It took years to finish the novel because the recent changes in Iran continually altered its last chapter. I wrote three other books while this one simmered on the backburner!

To find an agent was not difficult—unfortunately both my good New York agents had difficulty finding the right home for my novel. I am talking about great, professional people who knew their way around the industry and had years of experience. While I learned much from them and deeply respect their efforts, I realized that with our declining economy and the fact that I was an unknown writer, most publishers would be reluctant to give my novel a chance. The letters that came back were so complimentary that I call them "Regretful declines" instead of the more common name of "Rejection letters." Finally, much to my dismay and that of my agent, I decided to put it out there independently. I didn't want to have a book that looked self-published, so I started a small publishing company and made sure my novel received the best design and a highly professional layout. The success of this novel indicates that it was the right decision; however, the process entailed so much effort that I'm not sure I want to do the same with my next book.

What was the single most successful thing you did to promote your book?

Gathering a perfect team. Writers often express that a book is like their child. I now realize how true that is. Not only do we give birth to it, but we must raise it in the best possible way and give it the chance it deserves. Your post-publication work may be the hardest part of the job. While it is possible to do the work alone, the process is more pleasant—not to mention much easier—with help. By *team* I mean designers, web experts, and marketing advisors. Not only did I have the best writing community to share their experiences with me, I was also lucky to receive help from my talented children.

My daughter Lilly is my attorney and marketing advisor. I owe much of my success to her expertise and guidance. My other daughter, Susie, is a successful artist/designer/illustrator. Even though her art involves an entirely different field, she didn't hesitate to offer Mom a huge favor. Not only did she design the cover—using one of my own paintings—but she also selected the paper and font and supervised the layout. The cover design of *Sky of Red Poppies* placed second in the Benjamin Franklin Awards for 2011. Susie went a step further and designed my posters, flyers, postcards, and bookmarks. My son, Cyrus John, is not only a talented musician but also a computer wizard! His supervision on my new website, mass e-mails, and announcements have been among the best gifts I have ever received. To this day, it is with my children's help that I manage to cope with my immense electronic handicap! When I run out of energy, the three are there to cheer me on. I realize that not everyone is blessed with such an inside team, but don't underestimate the talents and power of good friends and colleagues. Help is all around you, and promotion doesn't have to cost a fortune.

What aspect of book promotion surprised you the most?
The friends it brought me. I had a feeling my children, family, and friends would like my story. What I didn't expect was an entire city that would embrace my work—*Sky of Red Poppies* was chosen for *One Book, One San Diego* in 2012. Something about this novel resonated with readers, and they liked, chose, and promoted it. I would go for a talk at a library branch, and someone who had already heard me and bought a copy would return to hear me again and to buy a stack as gifts. People came to talk to me, not just as an author but as someone they could relate to. Young students saw me as proof that dreams do come true, other writers affectionately called me

their "poster child," and teachers invited me to their classes. Having lived the life of a hermit during those writing years, I am overwhelmed with the number of friends I've made since the launch of this novel.

What was your biggest marketing challenge?
Reviews, or rather their scarcity. As if by a secret pact, none of the major publications will review an independent publisher's product. After a few good reviews and several interviews, I noticed how, following each bit of publicity, the sale rates rose. It took me a while to realize that none of the major publications had approached me for a review. Finally, an honest editor from *LA Times*—who had liked my talk—regretfully informed me that their protocol prevented him from reviewing my work. Such discrimination didn't surprise me, but I'll have to admit, it was most disappointing. I can only imagine how high my novel would have soared with a review in the *Washington Post* or *New York Times*.

Yet my book became a 2012 *One Book, One San Diego* pick without such help and gained its fame on its own merit. Before the nomination of my novel, I didn't know anything about the selection process for One Book. I recently learned that the primary selection is done through a committee. The most interesting finding for me was that on their first meeting in 2011, two of the committee members—none of whom knew me—brought my book to the table! The nomination alone was a huge success because suddenly I was up there with two of the best contemporary writers. I owe my success to KPBS, the San Diego Library, and my San Diego community.

Further promotion came from many sources. I think we are often so caught up in our projects that we may underestimate the power of the media and the Internet. To keep a blog, update your website, and post to both Facebook and Twitter is a great start. But once you have presented your work, there are many online reviewers who are willing to offer their support and spread the word among their followers. As I mentioned before, there is much more to raising this "child" than we presume. If you can't keep up with all the work, then find a good babysitter and make sure the child is in safe hands! Find someone who will update your posts and keep the momentum going. I did most of mine, but I must admit, any time I slacked, one of my team members was there to set me straight. Also, make a habit of sharing the success of your friends and colleagues. You should never be too busy to help a friend. Write a blurb, show up for their readings, and post reviews on their Amazon pages. Remember, you are only as strong as your community.

What advice do you have to offer new authors?
Never forget a good lesson. Years ago, I used to play in a tennis league, and my coach told me it was wrong to worry about a shot I had missed as it would be sure to affect my game. "You are only as good as your next shot," he said. I think of that often. In this life we can only go forward. You failed? Try again. Your agent isn't who you'd like? Switch to someone you can relate to. Your story sags in the middle? Go back and fix it. There's always a solution for a problem, and it's up to you to find it.

Remember that having a platform may well be the most important aspect of a writer's success. Remember all those discussions in your writing class and how the teacher said, "Write what you know best"? A successful writer needs a strong platform. This comes to your aid when you present your book. Complete knowledge of your subject is essential when you begin to promote your project. To fall back on our familiar metaphor, know your child well before attending that parent-teacher conference. Write with passion and become one with your work because your readers see you and your book as one.

And finally, be sincere. *Sky of Red Poppies* was my tribute to my culture, my motherland, and the people who had left an indelible image in my heart and soul. But more than anything, I wrote it for my best friend and am pleased that the outcome presents a universal story of friendship. I was honest both in my feelings and my limitations. The feelings were so true and raw that from time to time I cried while writing it. In the words of Sa'adi, the Persian poet of the thirteenth century, "A word that rises from one heart has no choice but to settle onto another." Today my emotions are transferred to readers, which may well be the reason behind their strong support.

When you are close to your subject, there's no need to rehearse, prepare notes, or review your speeches. Sincerity will provide the courage you need to speak before an audience, be it five people or five hundred. It will also enable you to answer their questions with more confidence. If there are facts that you don't know, admit it with honesty. Readers often ask me questions about Iran's political conflicts. I don't mind telling them that after nearly forty years of life in the U.S., I am no more informed on the subject than they are, and that my knowledge mainly comes from our media. Readers are smart, and they respond well to candor. If you are devoted and if your work represents the true you, there's no need to write a speech. All you'll need to do is be yourself and relate to your audience, and I promise you the words will flow.

POET KELLI RUSSELL AGODON

Kelli Russell Agodon is the author of *Letters from the Emily Dickinson Room, Small Knots,* and *Geography.* She co-edited *Fire On Her Tongue: An eBook Anthology of Contemporary Women's Poetry.* Kelli is the editor of *Crab Creek Review* and the co-founder of Two Sylvias Press. Her third book of poems, *Hourglass Museum,* will be published in 2014. Visit her online at www.agodon.com.

Tell us about how your books came into the world.

Each book came about very differently, and all with the wonder if they'd ever be published.

My first chapbook, *Geography,* won the Floating Press Chapbook Prize in 2003. I had really started to question my work and whether I was writing well or making any sort of difference in the literary community. I told my husband, "Sometimes I think I'm just paying an extra tax to the post office by sending out all these submissions. What am I doing this for?" It was kind of a mini-meltdown where I was really wondering if I was a writer who'd ever get a book published, so I was very thankful when the news of this prize came to me.

A few months after that, I learned my full collection, *Small Knots,* was a finalist in the Cherry Grove Collection book prize and the editor wanted to publish it.

My second book, *Letters from the Emily Dickinson Room,* took a lot longer to get published and went through many rejections. I think I sent it out for at least four years, and it was probably rejected seventy times (about fifteen times a year). Much of the rejection happened because, in my excitement to be writing new poems, I began sending the book out before I should have. For the first two and a half years, it wasn't complete and was still a work-in-progress. However, I learned from each rejection, and each rejection gave me the time to make it stronger. In 2009, it was chosen by Carl Dennis for the White Pine Press Poetry Prize and then published in 2010.

The anthology I edited with Annette Spaulding-Convy came about because we were on a ferry ride home and were complaining about how hard it was to find poetry for our e-readers. We decided right then to create and edit *Fire On Her Tongue: An eBook of Contemporary Women's Poetry.* That e-book then created our small press, Two Sylvias Press. It's kind of amazing how these things happen … I live with the belief that "anything's possible if you don't know what you're doing."

What was the single most successful thing you've done to promote your books?
Oddly, I'm not sure I'd have any idea what *one* thing it is, but probably a coming together of many. Having my poem on Poetry Daily (www.poems.com) was a huge boost because poetry readers visit there daily, so I connected with a lot of people outside my area.

Another thing I did was send my book to ten random people. These can go to anyone, like a reader who sends me an e-mail saying they liked a poem of mine, or I may mail a copy off to Garrison Keillor for his "Writer's Almanac" radio show. I just like sending my book out into the world and seeing what happens—sometimes nothing, sometimes a lot.

From my ten-random-people experiment, my poem went on to be recited by Garrison Keillor on his radio show and then ended up in his *Good Poems for Hard Times* anthology. You never know what doors your book will push open, and it's a fun way to connect with others and send your work into the world.

What aspect of book promotion has surprised you the most?

I think I was most surprised when I found myself having fun doing it. When I hear "book promotion" or "marketing," I can get a knot in my stomach, as I have always hated anything to do with sales. However, when I view "book promotion" as what it is—sharing my work and meeting other creative people—I find the joy in it.

Many of the people who come to readings and poetry events are also writers themselves. I love meeting other writers and expanding my creative community, so realizing that there's a lot I like in promoting my book has been a nice surprise.

What is your biggest marketing challenge?

Myself. If anything gets in the way of marketing my book, it's me—worrying if I'm coming off as a "shameless self-promoter" or having to overcome shyness to ask for what I want. Everyone else has been fantastic in helping me get my book(s) out in the world, but if anyone gets in my way, it's usually me.

As co-founder of Two Sylvias Press, which publishes in electronic formats, how do you find marketing different than it is in the world of print?
Well, it's much harder to do book readings where audience members can't buy your book at the bookstore and then have the poets sign it! But otherwise a lot of it is the same as marketing a print book.

Right now, many people find out about new poets through the Internet, so letting people know about *Fire On Her Tongue* has been similar. We also used press releases, postcards, review copies—all of the same things I did or my publishers did with my print books.

What advice do you have to offer new authors?
1) If you're trying to publish your book, be persistent.

2) If you *have* a book published and are trying to market it, be polite and professional.

3) Use your newly acquired fame to help promote other writers you like. It's wonderful to support others, and having a book will give you the platform to help raise others up and share their work as well. Remember, we are a writing community full of readers and writers. Share the wealth with others, and let that good karma come back to you twofold.

4) Remember there is no one way to be a writer in the world. Try new things (make a book trailer, start a Facebook page) and find ways to promote your book that make you feel good. If you like working with people, see if you can volunteer

somewhere. Or visit someone's book group. Find ways to share your book with others that you enjoy.

5) Don't judge your success by your royalty check. We are artists first, and we can't judge our work by a dollar sign.

POET ELIZABETH AUSTEN

Elizabeth Austen is the author of *Every Dress a Decision*, a finalist for the Washington State Book Award, and two chapbooks, *The Girl Who Goes Alone* and *Where Currents Meet*. Her poems have appeared online (The Writer's Almanac, Verse Daily), and in journals including *Willow Springs, Bellingham Review*, the *Los Angeles Review*, and the *Seattle Review*, and anthologies including *Poets Against the War, A Face to Meet the Faces*, and *What to Read in the Rain*. Elizabeth produces literary programming for KUOW 94.9, a Seattle NPR affiliate.

What are some of the best ways an author can prepare for a live interview?

The most important thing is to spend some time beforehand thinking about what you want to say about your work. Imagine the interview is already over: What do you want to have said? What would you regret *not* saying?

Often, the person interviewing you will not have had time to read your book. So you need to be prepared with a short description of it. What's your book about? Why did you write it—what drew you to this subject matter? Is it a departure from your previous work, and if so, in what ways? Is there an interesting story about how it got published? Also think about what you want to say about how you got started writing and why you continue to do it.

You're essentially interviewer-proofing yourself. Hopefully you'll get an interviewer who is genuinely interested in you and your book, and will talk with you briefly before the interview starts about what he/she wants to discuss, but you can't depend on that.

Also, choose a couple of short excerpts or a few short poems that you might read aloud. What would provide a good introduction to the book? Practice reading aloud, and practice giving a concise introduction to what you're going to read.

If you have time, I recommend listening online to an example or two of your interviewer's program, so that you'll have a sense of what to expect in terms of tone and approach. Does this interviewer tend to ask more about craft and process, or about the backstory of the book or individual poems? Is the interviewer looking for anecdotes and stories? Does it seem like the interviewer has actually read the book?

I'm a great believer in preparing for anything, and then letting go of the preparation during the interview so you can respond to what's actually happening in the conversation. The most important thing is to be present. In the moment, approach it like you would any conversation with someone you care about—by listening and responding as honestly and generously as you can.

What if you're asked a question you can't (or don't wish to) answer?
If there are topics that you consider off-limits for the interview, try to come to an understanding about that with

your interviewer beforehand. If that's not possible, and a question seems intrusive or inappropriate to you, then take a deep breath and pose a different question to yourself, and answer that. Perhaps something like this: "For me, the real question is … " or "Well, I'm more interested in why … "

More often, it's a matter of a question catching you off guard than being inappropriate. Remember that it's perfectly fine to admit that you don't know the answer to a question. Perhaps the interviewer is suggesting something you've never considered before—just say so, and answer as fully as you can in the moment.

Do you have any broadcasting secrets for how to sound your best on the radio?
Well, they're not really secrets, but here are a couple of things to keep in mind. Try to get a good night's sleep, but don't freak out if you don't. For a variety of reasons that I won't go into here, I got less than four hours of sleep the night before I was interviewed on KUOW along with former poet laureate Billy Collins. I think I was actually too sleep-deprived to be nervous. However, I don't recommend this as a tactic, in general!

Of course, avoid dairy products for a few hours before and don't drink so much caffeine that you're twitchy. Keep your feet on the ground, remember to breathe, and most of all, treat the interview like you would a conversation—that means listening as well as speaking.

And on a technical note—before the interview starts, try to get a chance to talk into the microphone to make sure you're not too close or too far away.

Do you have advice for writers who get nervous before interviews?

Does anybody not get nervous before interviews? I know I do—whether I'm the interviewer or the interviewee. I have a mantra that I tell myself before I perform, and it's equally true when I'm interviewing or being interviewed: "The performance requires me, but it's not about me." In other words, I need to show up and be present, but the focus is on the work, not on me (even if I'm talking about my process or any autobiographical connection to the material). The point—whether in a performance or an interview—is to help the reader connect to the work. When I keep my focus on that, my anxiety is much less likely to take over. Another thing to remember is that the nervousness is a kind of necessary fuel.

What if you make a mistake on the air—is there any way to overcome that?

The fact is that the best radio is made when people are actually talking to each other—so that means they're going to make mistakes sometimes. If you misstate something and realize it on the air, just correct yourself. If the interview is being recorded, and you stumble while reading an excerpt from your book, just back up to the beginning of a sentence—they can correct it in the editing room. If you're reading live, just go with it, like you would at a live reading. You don't have to be perfect. You just have to be you (hmmm—and maybe that's the scarier prospect!).

AUTHOR JACKIE BOUCHARD

Jackie Bouchard is the author of *What the Dog Ate*, first published as an e-book and later in paperback. Jackie has lived in Bermuda, Canada, and the east coast of the U.S. and now lives in San Diego with her husband and her rescue pup, Rita. Her work has been published in *San Diego CityBeat* and the San Diego Writers Ink anthology, *A Year in Ink, Vol. 3*. Visit her online at www.jackiebouchard.com.

Tell us about how your book came into the world.

A few years ago, my hubby got a very demanding job and started working tons of hours. He rarely got home before 8 p.m. or even later, and I needed something to do with myself at night. Rather than frequenting dive bars, I signed up for "An Introduction to Creative Writing."

I got the idea for the opening of *What the Dog Ate* from an episode of *Emergency Vet* on Animal Planet. A dog on the show had eaten something like nine squeaky toys, and I thought, "What if a dog ate something that was evidence?" The idea of a dog eating panties that didn't belong to the owner hit me, and the story flowed from there.

Over the course of the class I signed up for, I wrote a short story based on that idea. The instructor encouraged me to explore the characters and turn it into a manuscript, so I thought, "What the heck." I signed up for more classes and worked away, turning that short story into a novel.

What made you decide to publish in e-book format?
Way back in the spring of 2008 when my manuscript was "finished" (I say that in quotes because I was too much of a writing/publishing virgin at the time to realize how much work it still needed), I sent it off to an agent I really liked whom I'd met at a writing conference the previous year. I'd read a key scene in a session she led, and she'd invited me to submit it to her when it was done. She rejected it, but sent me some great suggestions. So I worked hard, sent it back to her in the fall of 2008, and she signed me! Oh, what exciting times ... and then, the market crashed. By the time we finished putting the final tweaks on the manuscript, we were pitching it in early 2009. Not great timing in any industry, let alone publishing. Even though I got good rejections, they were still rejections. I tried to put the book out of my head and get on with the next one. Then, in January of 2012, I had dinner with my agent, and she encouraged me to self-publish it. Another author she represented had self-published his first book, so with his guidance I was on my way to formatting and self-publishing my first e-book.

What was the biggest challenge in finding your audience?
For me, it was not getting discouraged! Probably most new authors, especially those of us who are self-/indie-published,

have read the advice that one of the best ways to market your book is to approach book bloggers. If the book bloggers love your book, they'll talk it up, their readers will buy it, and you're on your way.

On the face of it, that's fairly easy advice to follow, but when you actually start approaching the bloggers, you find most of the popular sites overwhelmed with requests. You try to do everything you can to get on their good side (don't send out a generic form e-mail, find out the blogger's first name and spell it correctly (!), be sure they're a fit for your book, etc.), and *still* you often don't hear back, or you hear back but they can't fit you in. Or they can fit you in, but they want to schedule your review eight months from now.

It's hard not to get discouraged in the face of that!

What are among the most successful things you've done to promote your book?

There are two main things I did that I'd say have been the biggest help in promoting my book. One was something I did on my own, and the second was in conjunction with a popular e-reader site.

The first thing I did (after I got discouraged about all the rejections or delays from book bloggers), was to realize there was another way: connecting with dog lovers. I got the idea by contemplating who my ideal reader would be and where I could find that person. I think my book appeals mostly to dog-loving women in their thirties or forties. I had started my own dog blog a year or so earlier (to chronicle my fifteen-month-old dog's journey with bone cancer), so I knew some other dog bloggers, and I knew they tended to mainly be women. I searched on "dog blogs" and "book reviews" and found a few pet blogs that occasionally included book reviews. I started following those bloggers, getting to know them, leaving comments. When I had a sense for whether or not I thought they might like my novel, I approached them about reviewing the book. I not only had a better success rate with the dog bloggers than the book bloggers (about 75 percent agreed to review the book, host a giveaway, or let me do a guest post, versus less than half of the book bloggers), but, in general, they reviewed the book much more quickly, and, on the whole, they tended to "LOVE" the book, in all caps even!

Continuing to try to connect with dog lovers, I approached several dog magazines and online e-zines. These were a harder sell, since they tend to only feature traditionally published books that are available everywhere, or some prefer nonfiction books. I came across the NBC Petside.com site and noticed they had written up some pieces on "dog lit" (as I like to call dog-friendly fiction—I'm hoping it'll catch on!). I reached out to them via the CONTACT US form. I never heard anything back, but in the meantime, I'd also reviewed their "about us" page and read the contributors' bios. For the ones that seemed like they might be my "ideal reader," I started following them on Twitter. One of them followed me back and saw the info about *What the Dog Ate* in my Twitter header. She messaged me asking for a review copy, so I sent one off to her. She ended up loving the book, and included it in NBC Petside's "Dog Books—Best of 2012" list.

The second thing I did was to have a 99-cent sale for my book as part of a "Bargain Book" promotion through Ereader News Today (ENT, www.ereadernewstoday.com). ENT has a huge following on their site and their Facebook page, and the two-day sale was a massive boost to my sales, briefly shooting *What the Dog Ate* up to the #1 Bestselling position on the Comic

Fiction list on Amazon. I even broke into the top 100 Kindle books in general. (I briefly experienced the heady joy of being a bestselling author! Amazon even slapped a "Bestseller" icon on the front of my book, if only for a short time.) This was all quite recently, so hopefully the momentum will continue. I'm already seeing more reviews coming in on Amazon, and I'm certain these most recent ones are attributable to the 99-cent sale.

What aspect of book promotion has surprised you the most?

The aspect that surprised me the most is that it really can be as simple as making new connections. I'm not a good salesperson, especially when it comes to selling myself. I thought I would really hate this whole marketing/promo part of the writing "biz." Sometimes I do start to get down about the business side of writing, but then I remember to just try to get out there and connect with people—other writers, other book lovers, and other dog lovers. If I approach it with that mindset, it makes me feel that it's something I can accomplish, and actually enjoy doing.

What advice do you have to offer new authors?

Don't get discouraged. It can all seem pretty overwhelming sometimes, and connecting with readers takes a lot of time and energy. Sometimes it's easy to think, "I give up. I'd rather be an unknown writing hermit than e-mail yet another blogger." But don't despair! Just keep chipping away. One of the great things about e-books, print-on-demand, and this new publishing world is that our books won't be pulled from store shelves if they aren't selling in order to make room for new inventory. It might take months and months for readers to find you, but your e-book will be there, ready and waiting, when they do.

Also, get in touch with other authors—especially those who are roughly at the same stage on the publishing path that you are (these folks will be a huge support system), as well as maybe a short way ahead of you on the path (these folks will be a wealth of knowledge). I reached out to a few authors who were about a year ahead of me in publishing their books (picking people who I could see were having success), and they were very helpful in sharing marketing tips.

How did you decide to publish a print version of your book?

At first I had only planned to publish an e-version. I released it in March of 2012, and it wasn't until a few months later that I started realizing a print version would be good to have—primarily for promotional purposes. I contacted an author that I'd "met" through Facebook and asked her advice. She said she sells many, many more e-books than print books, but the print books definitely help with promotion. In July of 2012, I published the print version of *What the Dog Ate* through CreateSpace. Print-on-demand makes it fairly easy and affordable to publish a paperback. It's not like the old days (a mere few years ago) when you had to order a thousand-book print run and worry about where you were going to store them all.

I found the CreateSpace option to be a great way to go. Other than paying my cover designer to add in a back cover and spine, I did everything else myself (in terms of formatting) so it was very inexpensive to get the book up and ready for sale.

As with the author whose advice I sought, I've sold very few print books compared to e-books, but the promotional opportunities it's allowed me have been great. (Plus, it's just plain fun to hold your own book in your hands, and being able to give people signed copies is an added bonus!) For example, Goodreads will only allow authors to do giveaways of print books. I did a two-week giveaway for two signed copies, and over one thousand people entered. Of those, four hundred of them added my book to their "Want to Read" list. It was a quick, cheap, and easy way to get my book in front of a lot of eyeballs. Also, the Petside.com contributor who asked me to send her a copy of the book specifically asked for a print copy. Luckily, I was able to send one right off to her. Finally, some reviewers and contests won't accept e-books. It's definitely worth it to have print books available!

Author Promotion

PUBLICIST ALICE B. ACHESON

Alice B. Acheson has decades of experience as an editor, publicist, marketing specialist, and publishing consultant. She works with authors, illustrators, and photographers as well as large and small publishers. She lives in Friday Harbor, Washington, and can be contacted at AliceBA@aol.com. Visit her online at http://sites.google.com/site/AliceBAcheson.

Publishing has changed so much over the years. Today, what are an author's biggest challenges, as well as the biggest advantages?

Publishing has always been challenging for authors. How to find an agent? How to find a (reputable) publisher? What is the most important function that a publisher can provide? Today, those questions are expanded to: Should I self-publish? Should I instead pay a company to produce my book?

There is general confusion about those last two questions. A self-published book is one for which the author has created a publishing company and obtains the ISBN (International Standardized Book Number) for that book. A company that an author pays to produce his or her book obtains the ISBN, which *might* cause a problem later for the author.

These last two methods have produced a great challenge. In the 1970s, when I entered publishing, there were 50,000 titles published each year. That was true until about 2000. Since then, that number has exploded to more than 200,000 titles per year and, generally, books produced by these two methods have not had professional input. Therefore, due to time demands (and other concerns), book reviewers and bookstores don't have a way of judging those additional 150,000 titles and will favorably view the traditionally published book over other titles and will know that their audiences can obtain those books through normal distribution channels.

Of course, there have been hugely successful books that have been self-published or produced by companies that charge for publishing services. However, reading the stories of those successes, it becomes evident that those authors dedicate "every waking moment" to the marketing of their books, which many authors cannot do or don't have the expertise to do.

What do you think are the most important things an author needs to consider for successful book promotion?
A. The verbal pitch. That sounds like a simplistic answer, but all authors should be talking to "everyone" about their prospective book as soon as the concept has been formulated. You never know to whom you might be talking: someone who can refer you to an agent, someone with a marvelous—but different—contact, someone who will offer to read your manuscript and provide much needed feedback (not just "I loved it"), someone who can provide a benefit, a market, an opportunity that you never envisioned.

That 30-second pitch should include:

- The title
- Genre
  - Fiction—mystery, historical novel, sci-fi, short story collection, etc.
  - Nonfiction—self-help, biography, autobiography, memoir, essays, etc.
  - Poetry—epic, narrative, etc.
  - Children's book—picture book, first reader, young adult, etc.
- Highlights of the book (not all are appropriate), such as:
  - Benefits—self-help, spiritual, etc.
  - Interesting research, travel, equipment used
  - Reason or inspiration for writing the book
  - Fascinating characters or interaction among them
  - Conflict (in novels) and theme or plot
  - Type of poetry
  - Target age for your children's book
  - Type of illustration or photography—let us "see" the picture
- Exciting news (again, not all are appropriate), such as:
  - An agent is interested and/or a publisher has asked for the complete manuscript

- A famous writer has supplied praise

- At a writers' conference, you pitched your book to five interested agents (or editors)

- A magazine is going to print a poem, a chapter, an excerpt

- A movie company/TV network has asked to see the manuscript

As you tell more and more people about your book, your pitch will change, as you will notice points that don't "sell," are confusing, or need more explanation. You also should be adding names of interested people to the database I will next discuss.

B. If you are including all genres, the most important thing an author needs for successful book promotion is distribution. Obviously, a nonfiction book is "easier," because the market can be better defined. Additionally, if the book is a series, the second or third book will be more successful, thanks to the market found for the first title.

However, all genres have nonfiction elements, be they their themes, locations, the interests of the protagonists, etc. All authors should update the list of people they know—from their hometown, college, work, church, organizations, etc. They are the first people who will be interested in what you are doing. By *update* I mean e-mail addresses, of course, but also phone numbers, addresses, etc., in a database that can be sorted for geographic location.

C. The more you learn about the publishing profession, the more success you will have. I'm always surprised by authors who have published a book or two and have no idea when galleys for their next book should be available, who the sales rep is, how their local booksellers association can help, how they could become a "partner" with their publisher in the marketing of their book. A valuable education can be obtained by reading *Publishers Weekly*, subscribing to Shelf Awareness [free at www.shelf-awareness.com], visiting an independent bookstore once a week, attending writers' conferences, etc.

How does a publicist help expand an author's reach?
That could fill this book. A publicist can be of enormous help—if you and she (most are female) agree on what would be the best areas on which she should focus her efforts and if she specializes in book publicity. That seems obvious, but many authors choose a publicist who has previously handled a well-known celebrity. Most likely, that publicist does not know the time line and special characteristics of book publicity.

I provide my classes with twelve functions that could/should be accomplished for a successful book. Some depend on the topic of the book or the author. Some books, for example, are not suited for op-ed essays, and some authors are not capable of writing quickly and well about a topic in the news. But all authors should be aware of the possibility and how to complete the task—if possible.

Reviewers generally prefer to talk to a publicist rather than the author, but the author can assist in making that conversation more successful.

I'm sure you know how much impact an award can make on sales of your book, but you need to research the many awards, know when to apply, and know which can only be submitted by the publisher. These are just three of the twelve functions, and a publicist can assist with all twelve.

What questions should an author ask a publicist he/she is considering working with?

You should ask which books/authors she has handled recently and what she did for those authors, whether she provides a contract stating agreed functions to be performed, whether she will share the names of people contacted and their response, etc. Some publicists will teach you how to publicize your book effectively, which is less expensive than her doing it. Some publicists work only with big-name authors and big-name publishers, some focus on book tours, some focus on encouraging book reviewers to consider a title, some specialize in arranging bookstore events, and some do all these functions. Again, it's a matter of education. For example, I ask a potential client what he/she believes would be most beneficial for the book. If we agree on that first topic, we can then proceed to other considerations.

What should an author expect to pay when working with an independent publicist?

I believe some require a six-month retainer at $5,000 per month. Others charge by the function. I charge by the hour as so many clients are with me for years and pop up with a question or a project, and I can't determine ahead of time how much they know or need.

Publicity-wise, what are the differences between working with self-published and/or small-press authors versus authors who publish with one of the big New York houses?

There are four differences. First is the distribution capabilities of established publishers. Second is the support staff that can aid the publicist. Third is the additional contacts the established publishers have. Fourth, as I've said before, the lack of education that most self-published and/or small-press authors possess.

In your experience, what are the most common mistakes authors make, and how can they avoid them?
They wait too long to begin marketing their book, and/or they "telescope" the time needed to produce their book, thereby eliminating marketing possibilities.

I'm beginning to sound like a broken record (yes, a cliché), but educating themselves about the entire publishing process will ease and maybe eliminate those mistakes.

Can you share one or two of your biggest success stories?
At one time I handled the publicity for four books (one literary fiction, one commercial fiction, one literary nonfiction, one commercial nonfiction) that simultaneously were on the bestseller list of the *New York Times*. Obviously, that was exciting, especially when one of the four "fell off" the list and a debut novel I handled replaced it on the list, thereby expanding my successes to all the basic genres.

However, my biggest success was *Old Turtle* by Doug Wood, published by Pfeiffer-Hamilton in Duluth, Minnesota. They had published many books but never a children's picture book, and none had been marketed nationally. However, the publisher believed in the book, hired professionals to assist them, and listened to the advice that was offered.

For example, they wanted to send Doug on a book tour immediately, but I said they weren't ready because the publishing world did not know them, nor did the bookstores. They agreed to wait four months while I educated the staff, we prepared appropriate materials, we contacted the stores, etc.

There were many other times when I as the publicist wanted to do one thing and the publisher—for a variety of reasons—was not able to concur. However, we compromised, and the publicity campaigns were successful. The book sold 800,000 copies and won the American Booksellers Association "Book of the Year," and I won the *Literary Market Place* Outside Services Award for Advertising, Promotion, and Publicity. Subsequently the title, plus now eight similar books, were sold to Scholastic, where *Old Turtle* is still published, twenty years after it first appeared.

Are you available for questions from authors?

Yes, if you have a problem that can be discussed in fifteen minutes, I'm happy to share my experience. My e-mail address is AliceBA@aol.com. When I answer your e-mail, I will probably ask that you call me at a mutually arranged time. That way, I am able to access my computer for information you might need at the same time we are speaking and can hear if you really understand the answer or are just saying "yes," when you really need the explanation rephrased.

Obviously, if our chat needs greater expansion, then it is time to discuss my fee, whether you believe the money and estimate of time are appropriate, and whether our collaboration will be useful.

PHOTOGRAPHER ROSANNE OLSON

Rosanne Olson began her career as a photojournalist after receiving her master's degree in journalism. Since starting Rosanne Olson Photography, she has photographed portraits as well as advertising campaigns for the New York City Ballet, Seattle Opera, Seattle Symphony, and Children's Hospital. Her award-winning work has been featured in *Communication Arts* and *More* magazine, among others, and she is the author of the book *This is Who I Am*.

What do you think makes a good author photo?

The photograph needs to convey how the author wants to portray himself/herself. Usually that means approachable, intelligent, engaging. Some people are more dramatic in how they want to be seen. Some are more friendly or sophisticated.

What advice can you offer to writers who are nervous about having their photos taken?

People come to me with varying degrees of "nervousness"

about how they look and how they "photograph" ("No one has ever taken a good photo of me" is a common complaint). This is very natural. My approach to get people to relax is to spend time talking to my clients before I pick up my camera. I also will likely read some of their work prior to the session. I make recommendations about clothing and makeup, and then, as the session proceeds, share some of the digital images with the client. I like to make them feel that they are in competent and compassionate hands with something that is very precious to them. After the session, I get them to sit with me to edit the photos to make sure they get the look they want.

What are the biggest mistakes authors make when it comes to their photos?

Sometimes people come here with too much makeup on. Or they bring their clothing stuffed into a bag so everything is wrinkled. Believe me, not just authors do this but lots of people. It is actually pretty amusing except for the fact that clothing then needs to be pressed or steamed here. Aside from that, people are usually willing to trust me to do the best possible job that I can with them. It is an exquisite collaboration.

What should an author expect to pay for a professional author photo?

Photographers' fees vary across the country, but most charge somewhere between $150 and $2,500. If you pay the least amount possible for a photo you may get something okay. Or even just fine. But will it work for years to come? I try to work with people and their budgets. It is definitely an important investment.

Do you recommend color or black-and-white for author photos—and why?

Things are shot digitally these days, so all images come out in color, and it takes an extra step to convert them to black-and-white or sepia. That said, I think color conveys more because it is, well, color.

Do you have any recommendations for authors who are looking for a photographer? What questions should they ask?

An author photo is an important piece of one's "brand." If you have a photo you like, you can use it for years. When people see it they will think of you and of your work. I think of some of the famous, famous photos of people like Ernest Hemingway and Raymond Carver and how they convey so much at a glance. Pick your photographer by looking at the photographer's website and perhaps talking on the phone. Also, ask for references from other artists and authors who have been photographed by that person.

BOOK BLOGGER SERENA M. AGUSTO-COX

Serena M. Agusto-Cox is a poet and amateur photographer who lives outside Washington, D.C. She has published poetry in *Beginnings, LYNX, Muse Apprentice Guild, The Harrow, Poems Niederngasse, Avocet,* and *Pedestal,* as well as an essay in *Made Priceless* by H.L. Hix. Her blog, Savvy Verse & Wit (www. savvyverseandwit.com), features writing critiques; book reviews of poetry, fiction, and nonfiction; and conference/ book event news.

How did your blog first come about?
My blog, Savvy Verse & Wit, began because I wanted to talk about poetry—writing and reading it—and I wanted to keep a record of my thoughts on the books I read. That was back in 2007, and to be honest, the name came out of my love of verse and the words *savvy* and *wit.*

How many book review pitches do you receive each week?
I did not receive many pitches at all in the beginning, but now, after five years, I receive about ten to fifteen pitches per day from a variety of publishers, authors, and publicists. Some of these pitches are well within the types of books I

read, which isn't really hard since I'm an eclectic reader. I love poetry above all else, but that's closely followed by literary and historical fiction. I read a bit of nonfiction/biography/memoir, but I am pickier about my nonfiction reading. The other pitches I receive are far outside and are usually turned down quickly.

I have a standard response that I crafted to send to everyone who requests a review. It's very simple, but I make sure to change the name so that it addresses each person individually. This standard response is for books I'm not interested in at all, but I will make more personal responses for books I'm interested in but may not have a certain opening they are looking for in terms of reviews. I will often suggest a different time frame, a guest spot/interview, or a giveaway. There are certain things that get deleted without a response because they are automatic lists that are sent out to everyone, it seems, and don't require a response, and there are several publicists who have said I don't need to respond unless it's a go.

How many are from authors versus publishers?
I think I get a list from about three to four publishers per month with a list of upcoming titles, which are usually broken down into two-month batches. The rest are from authors or their publicists, plus the online book tour companies.

Do you pay closer attention to pitches from book tour companies than pitches from authors or publishers? Do you think they offer any advantages for authors from your perspective as a blogger?
I don't necessarily pay closer attention to online book tour companies, but there are some that I've worked with over the years that know my tastes and will pitch books I cannot refuse.

I think what tour companies do for an author is guarantee a certain amount of coverage within a certain time frame—i.e., in line with a paperback or hardback release, providing coverage before, during, and after a launch. I also find that some of the tour companies have a certain group of bloggers that they work with who provide the kind of social media interaction that authors/publishers are looking for that they might not get on their own. I don't necessarily call what I get from these tour companies *pitches*. Mostly, I receive a list of books and authors with synopses and links from the tour firm, and I respond with which books I want to tour on my blog. There are great number of tour companies out there, though none exclusively for poetry.

I'm also more out of the norm, probably, because I tend to like firm deadlines for book reviews, etc. I think it's the day job and its deadline environment. I like structure. As a poet, I find I get distracted without structure—whether it's artificially created by me or by a deadline I know is coming. If I have a more fluid deadline, it's easier for me to push it off and read something that's grabbing my attention at the moment.

How do you decide which books to review? Do you have any guidelines regarding self-published versus traditionally published books?
I generally do not accept self-published books unless they have gotten good reviews previously, are highly recommended (by a friend or an author I trust), or are on subjects that highly interest me. One self-published book that I took right away because of the subject was *Across the Mekong River* by Elaine Russell. This novel was about Vietnam and was recommended by a friend. I also rarely accept e-books for review unless the author has no time frame for the review or any expectations time-wise because I'm a slower reader on Kindle than I

am in traditional book form. I tend to get more distracted with electronic books, finding that my mind wanders to the television or other pursuits.

In terms of the traditionally published books, here are some rough guidelines I use:

- Is it an author I've already read and enjoyed?
- Is it poetry? Is it non-rhyming poetry? If not, is it rhyming poetry that is not trite or elementary?
- Is it a Jane Austen–based book or spin-off?
- Is it about Vietnam, WWI, WWII, the Cold War, or other wars of interest? What's the angle—home base versus battlefront?

For other types of fiction and nonfiction, the book's synopsis has to catch my eye in some way—whether it's a dysfunctional family, a mystery/suspense novel with a different premise, or something about Ireland, Spain, Brazil/South America, or Portugal—if it catches my eye, I'll generally take it, depending on the review time frame.

Also, I tend to turn down more than I accept these days as I have a toddler and a full-time job to pay the bills, so I try to keep scheduled reviews to one per week, leaving me more time to read some other books I've been neglecting or bring news to the audience about D.C. events and conferences.

What tips do you have for authors approaching book bloggers?

- My rule of thumb is always be professional and address the book blogger by name.

- Always check for a review policy; mine is here: http://savvyverseandwit.com/policies/review-policy.
- Don't beg, and *never* say, "I know you don't read _____, but you'll love my book."

Those are the general guidelines, but I also prefer pitches that follow this format:

- Pitches should contain the time frame for review; the book title, author, and synopsis; what images/videos/audio you would like included, and whether the author is available for interviews or guest posting opportunities.
- Additionally, publishers interested in sponsoring giveaways should include information about how many copies and any shipping restrictions.

What other options do you offer authors and publishers in addition to reviews, and should an author inquire about this when proposing a review?
I love hosting guest posts about writing spaces, including photos of the desk, views, inspirational tokens, etc., or guest posts about writing habits and schedules.

I do love interviews if I've read the book before or if it's a poet. I think the poetic process is different from fiction writing for some, or at least that's how readers often view it, so I like to shed light on that.

I've also done giveaways sponsored by authors, publishers, and on my own (though this can be costly for me if I cover the shipping); hosted excerpts and review quotes; and posted readings/videos with giveaways, etc. Authors and publishers should inquire about other opportunities as well. I'm pretty open to anything authors/publishers want to try, especially if the content is unique to the blogger community. I don't like to post content that I've already seen all over the book blogger community.

Events

EVENT MANAGER SUSAN MCBETH

Photo credit: Paul Brody

Susan McBeth is the founder and owner of Adventures By the Book (www.adventuresbythebook.com), which provides opportunities for readers to connect with authors through events and worldwide travels. She has worked as an event coordinator for more than twenty years, including as director of events and marketing at an independent bookstore, and has hosted events ranging from small, intimate gatherings for debut authors to large-scale events with high-profile and bestselling authors.

In what ways can nontraditional book events be good for sales and exposure?

Nontraditional book events are a fabulous way to increase sales and exposure for a variety of reasons. Keep in mind that the most successful events are those in which the author and the reader make a connection on some level. And when that magical connection occurs, you are more likely to generate increased book sales and exposure, as these readers will want to share with others the "experience" they just had.

To understand the value of a nontraditional book event, it is helpful to first envision a traditional bookstore lecture event, as this has been the standard and most popular model for many years. Typically, an author speaks to a group of readers in a more formalized setting, perhaps includes a short reading and/or Q&A, and then signs books. While bookstore events certainly can offer an enriching experience, in that setting, a connection most often will occur only when the author is charismatic and/or possesses the ability to engage an audience about his or her book.

Obviously there are readers who attend these events and purchase books because they are interested in the topic or are fans of a particular author. But make no mistake about it; there is a direct correlation between how engaged an audience is and how many books they will purchase after an event, regardless of the topic and regardless of how well known the author is. In fact, many times customers specifically choose not to purchase a book until after they have heard the author speak.

What a nontraditional event can offer an author, then, is the ability to increase the odds of making a connection with their readers beyond just through an engaging talk. And, just like in Las Vegas, when you increase your odds, your chance of winning also increases. And winning means more book sales and more exposure.

What are a few examples of non-bookstore events an author might try?

The best kind of nontraditional book event is one that is a good fit for an author's particular book, keeping in mind that the primary goal is to make a connection with the reader.

For example, say you have written a lighthearted, fun piece of fiction. Since the best way to connect is to envision what it is you want your readers to feel or experience when they read your book, try to anticipate your demographic. In this case, your audience will likely consist of women who want to laugh and be entertained. A happy hour event would be a great fit, then, because it has the same goals in mind. And if you are not an experienced or naturally gifted speaker, sipping a glass of wine and sitting informally amongst a group of readers is much less intimidating and more natural than lecturing in a more formal setting, and allows you an opportunity to chat one-on-one with readers. And when readers share a glass of wine and some appetizers, they already start off an event having a good time and possessing a mindset that the fun will continue, so your connection has begun even before you start speaking.

Nonfiction books can be a little trickier, as they are oftentimes of a more serious nature that may seem a better fit for a bookstore lecture event. However, there are opportunities available for nontraditional events as well, if you put some thought into how you can make that connection happen. Keep in mind that many nonfiction books are written to educate and raise awareness about a particular issue. If that is the case with your book, a great opportunity is to partner with a nonprofit organization that shares the same cause. The nonprofit may be looking for a speaker who can help them promote their cause, and you will benefit from having a built-in audience and reaching readers who are already interested in your topic.

These are just a few examples of some nontraditional events that can help you connect with your readers. Remember that this experience is supposed to be fun and meaningful for you, too. An audience can certainly intuit whether or not authors are enjoying their events, and if they are not, you can guarantee that no connection will be made, and book sales and exposure will suffer accordingly. But the great thing about nontraditional events is that there are no limits, so brainstorm away and create an event that is fun and meaningful for your reader and for you.

What are the best ways for writers to promote these events?

Promotion of your event may seem daunting at first, but it is crucial to the success of your event and likely will not be as difficult as you think. Think of your event promotion in terms of a set of concentric circles, and this will help you plan your campaign accordingly.

First and foremost, you are at the bull's-eye, the actual center of those circles, so the campaign must begin with you, which makes sense because you certainly cannot expect others to help promote your event if you are not doing so yourself. The goal is to make available and disseminate information about your event to as many readers as possible, including not only crucial details like date, time, venue, cost, etc., but other relevant and often overlooked information such as how readers register, where and how they may purchase books, and what they can expect from their experience.

Will this information be available on your website, through an invitation that you send out, on your social media platforms? Are there reviews available of your book, photos of you, and an image of your book jacket that you can include as well? Since there exists a fine line between including enough information without overdoing it and making your promotional materials verbose and complicated, it would be prudent to ask a few family members or close friends to check it out to gauge their reaction as readers before launching your campaign.

Once you have laid this groundwork, you can expand to the next closest circle, that of family, friends, and colleagues. After all, these are the close-reach people who are invested in you and want to see you do well. Do not be shy about asking them to spread the word to their friends and book clubs, whether it is by word of mouth, e-mail, or their own social media. As I built Adventures by the Book from ground zero, my first event consisted solely of a wonderful group of my girlfriends and colleagues, some of whom brought members of their family or book club members, and my following has grown organically from there.

The next concentric circle belongs to your immediate community. This is where you can post events at local libraries, community centers, on public event calendars, and at any other businesses or organizations with whom you have a connection or may have an interest in your event. Another benefit of a nontraditional event is that the hosting venue will be vested in ensuring its success, so ask them to help promote as well. Do not assume they will do this automatically, as they are understandably focused on running their day-to-day business, so make sure to provide them with the flyers or electronic data they need.

The outer circle consists of media, whether the traditional radio, television, and print media, or the social media variety. Do not be afraid to send out press releases for your event, and do not be afraid of jumping into the social media world, even if you have never before done so. Conduct a little research to see which are the most relevant social media at the time of your marketing campaign, as they change frequently and often.

While this is just a guideline to help get you started, there are myriad other opportunities available. Keep in mind your reading demographic and your own networking opportunities. And always remember that the amount of effort you put into promoting your event will bear a direct correlation to the success of your event.

Can you talk about one of your most successful/ memorable events and why it worked so well?

Adventures by the Book was founded on the premise that books connect people, so I measure the success of each nontraditional event I create by the level of connection that occurs. Perhaps the most memorable event was one that achieved success on all levels, which would not have been possible as a traditional bookstore event.

I was asked by a major publishing house to create an event for a relatively unknown (at the time) first-time author who wrote a book chronicling an immigrant who moved to the United States to escape the atrocities occurring in WWII-era Europe. This farmer used his last few dollars to purchase an inexpensive horse destined for the slaughterhouse but was able to turn the pathetic workhorse into a champion show horse.

Anticipating that horse lovers would be drawn to this event, I researched equestrian centers that might be conducive to hosting such an event. Some extensive research led me to a beautiful facility whose resident nonprofit partner raises funds to save horses from the slaughterhouse, horses exactly like the one featured in the book! In partnership, we created a fundraising event on the equestrian grounds, complete with breakfast buffet, facility tour, vendors, author talk and signing, and horse riding demo. The connection that occurred was magical indeed, enticing over 100 attendees, selling well over

100 books, earning rave author reviews, raising awareness and over $1,000 for the nonprofit organization, and offering all participants a unique, magical experience they will continue to talk about long after the event.

What are some good venues for events that allow an author to keep costs down?

If you are creative enough, most venues will work with you to keep costs down, as they want the event to be a success as much as you do. Look for venues that may be seasonal, and offer them business off-season or perhaps on a slow night. If you are working with a restaurant, many will offer a prix fixe menu or a happy hour menu for a discounted cost, in the hope that after your event, readers will stay and purchase a full meal or another glass of wine or two.

If you are looking for an inexpensive or no-cost venue, there are a multitude of libraries, community centers, and nonprofit organizations that may have space available for your event. It is important, however, to be a good community ambassador. If you are asking for a no-cost venue, offer something of value to the venue in exchange. For example, if you request to use a community room at your local library, offer to donate some books, or offer a free book talk at a later date to their book club.

Most importantly, do not dismiss any venue as a potential site for your event. I belong to a group of very savvy writers who once held a joint event in a hair salon that was a smashing success. Think about it: the salon received exposure to several hundred potential new customers by hosting an event during an evening they weren't even open. The authors brought in all the food and drink (purchased inexpensively themselves), the customers, and the marketing, so the salon's only out-of-pocket cost was to keep their lights on for a few extra hours.

What can an author expect to earn from an event?

Anticipating what an author can earn from an event is difficult to ascertain for a variety of reasons. There are authors who are savvy or creative enough, or who hire top-notch teams, to help them create revenue-generating events. In addition, there are other authors who are well-known or credentialed enough to demand an honorarium. As a general rule, however, most authors participate in events because they want to sell books, increase exposure, and build a platform that may down the road allow them to garner a regular, steady income. It is these authors whom I address here.

The most important thing to bear in mind when you set your expectations for an event, then, is to be realistic about what to expect. Successful events do not just magically occur. You must work hard to ensure the venue is a good fit and that the readers will have an experience that is memorable and rewarding. And you must promote, promote, promote!

There is no hard-and-fast rule about what to expect from an event, but, that being said, I personally use the one-percent rule. This is not a scientific measurement, but merely one I randomly set in my own head that gives me a more realistic sense of attendance. For example, if I partner with an organization that invites 1,000 people to my event, I feel comfortable expecting one percent of them, or ten, to attend the event. While this number may seem disappointing to those who dream of large events, remember two things: First, it is not about the number of attendees so much as it is about the connection. Second, this stresses the importance of inviting as many people as possible.

While the one-percent rule does not necessarily apply to family and friends, do be realistic about their attendance as well. They certainly want you to succeed and intend to support you, but when it comes down to it, they are like everybody else in that they have busy lives. If your event is scheduled for evening, they may be coming home from a long day at work, or seeing their spouses or children for the first time all day, and may just not feel up to going out again once they are home. If an author tells me that she is expecting fifty family members and friends to attend her event, I automatically cut that number in half.

To be realistic about attendance is to protect yourself from disappointment that you could project to readers at your event. Your goal is to do everything in your power to ensure a magical connection that will translate to book sales and greater exposure. And if it does not happen with one event, then take some thoughtful time to candidly assess what you can change for the next event. Remember that as your writing improves with each book, so, too, do your events. I have been hosting events for years and still learn something from every single one that I can improve upon for the next time. Do not let a disappointing event define you but rather allow it to teach you.

What do you think is the most important thing an author should keep in mind about finding new readers?
The most important thing for an author to keep in mind about finding new readers is not to assume anything.

Do not assume you can only reach local readers. Do you have long-distance friends and family that you visit? Why not have them help you set up an event in their area the next time you visit? Do you have contacts in another town that is too far away to visit? Send them a free copy of your book to read and review. And if they love your book, encourage them to set up a Skype event with their book club. With social media, you can reach and interest readers around the world.

Do not assume you cannot create a nontraditional event because you are not an experienced event planner. While it certainly is easier if you have event-planning experience, allow the learning curve to teach you at each event what works and what doesn't.

Do not assume readers will not come to your event because you are not well known or a bestselling author. If you create an event that readers want to experience, they will come.

Do not assume that the hard work is over because you have finished writing your book. If anything, the hard work is really just beginning. But if you work hard at promoting your book, the rewards are worth it, as there is nothing more satisfying than connecting people through books. So go out and create your own Adventure by the Book!

LIBRARY MANAGER AMY BLOSSOM

Amy Blossom is the manager at the Ashland Branch Library in Ashland, Oregon, and serves on the board of Friends of the Ashland Public Library. She is the host of *Open Books, Open Minds*, a local television program featuring interviews with authors from the Southern Oregon community and beyond.

What is the best way for a local author to approach his or her local or regional library?

A personal approach is much better than a cold e-mail. It's so easy to dismiss an e-mail, whereas a phone call or even stopping in allows for a personal connection. Then, after an initial conversation, I like to get a follow-up e-mail with all the details.

Also, authors should be sure to have a hook—a way to let us know what the book is about and why it would be of interest. We get a lot of requests, and it helps if your book or presentation has a fascinating angle to it.

If you're a new, unknown author or a self-published author, show that you are prepared to help bring in your own audience—if no one knows who you are, it's hard to get people to show up for an event. Joint events or group events have the potential to bring in more attendees, so you may want to team up with someone, not only to be sure you get enough people but also to broaden the exposure you'll get for your own book.

What common mistakes do authors make when approaching libraries?

One mistake is assuming they'll get paid. Some of the bigger libraries can offer honorariums, but often there's not enough in the budget for author appearances. Also, libraries have different policies on book sales, depending on the local jurisdiction, so this is something to ask about as well.

Authors also should know that they need to play a large role in promoting their events—sometimes we'll have no one show up, or only one person will come. So authors need to help get the word out, especially among their own friends and family, and to be prepared to reach out to the community to help bring people to the library.

Do you have any tips for how authors can help promote their events?

For one, sending e-mails to everyone in their contact list. Inviting everyone they know is very important—from fellow Rotary members, for example, to their local writers' association. One recent event we hosted had more than a hundred people because the authors got the word out to everyone they knew, and those people shared the news, and so on. Also, reach out to local radio programs and local media, and list your event on online calendars, from Craigslist to the local paper.

E-promotion is big—e-mail, social media, Facebook, Twitter—not only in advance, but also send a reminder out right before the event. Flyers are important, too—and authors can make these themselves if the library doesn't provide one. If it's a library program, there are usually library guidelines that must be followed in the publicity. Check that out with the librarian who will be hosting the event. Be sure your name is big, the time and date are in bold type, and that there's not too much text, which makes it look busy and doesn't usually get read by people walking past. Have a good image, like an author photo or book cover, and an artful, colorful design.

Always be willing to provide an author photo or book cover, and a bio. We do a press release for every event, but because we do so many, we often don't have the time to do special promotion for each one. This is where the author comes in. The author can ask the library for its press release, find out where it will be sent, and send it to places the library isn't.

It can be hard to predict what to expect in terms of turnout. Authors should make sure there's not a competing event in town. Each community is different. In some towns, everyone goes to sporting events on Saturdays, so that provides a lot of competition for an event. We notice that our community meeting room is usually open on Friday and Saturday nights because groups know that other events are going on, so they don't want to compete with that time. Winter nights can be difficult for us because a lot of our patrons don't like to drive in the dark in bad weather. And just when I say some day doesn't work, a large group will come and surprise us.

Ask the library if you can serve food or drinks; if it's allowed, serve something festive and, if possible, related to the book or the discussion.

What do libraries look for in an ideal author event?
A good crowd. Always be willing to e-mail all your contacts,

to contact the media, to put flyers up around town. It's especially helpful if you know someone connected to the media; often our press releases won't get noticed, but if an author knows someone at a radio station or newspaper, this helps. It's said that people don't read newspapers anymore, but I think they do—I always notice that when an event isn't listed in the paper, we get a smaller crowd. So it does make a difference.

More people will come to a workshop than a reading, so offering more than a reading can bring a better crowd. We have a lot of writers in town, so writing workshops always do well—as do cooking workshops. Any sort of "how to" event tends to do well; people like to come in and learn something. And if the author proposes a talk on an especially newsworthy or interesting topic, that's likely to be successful, too.

What's the best way for an author from another city or state to set up an event at a library?
Call first, then e-mail—or e-mail, then follow up with a call. Most libraries do quite a lot with local authors, so it's exciting to have authors from out of town asking about events.

What are some of the ways in which authors can support their local libraries?
Offering an event is in itself a great way to support the library. We also appreciate it when authors donate a copy of their book. Donating a copy along with ordering information, especially for self-published authors, is a wise idea because most libraries like to have local authors in their collections. Keep in mind that most libraries require that self-published books meet the same criteria as other books; for example, there needs to be a strong local interest, or the book should have received at least

two professional media or industry reviews. So it's a good idea to ask about such requirements when you consider donating a book to your local library.

I recently read a study noting that library users buy more books than any other type of book buyers. People often don't think of library users as big buyers, but being big readers in general, they are. So even if you may not sell a lot of books at an event, just by being there, you can still gain readers down the road.

EVENT COORDINATOR NAN MACY

Nan Macy is writing a nonfiction book about peace work during World War I. Previously, she coordinated all aspects of the 250-300 author events hosted annually by Village Books. An alumna of the writing residency program at Hedgebrook, she currently serves on its Alumnae Leadership Council. She is a founding organizer of the Chuckanut Writers Conference and holds an M.A. in American Studies and an M.A. in English with an emphasis on Composition and Rhetoric.

When is the best time for a writer to begin thinking about author events?

Before finishing the manuscript. If having one or more author events is something a writer is interested in, then it's vital to be thinking about this en route to publishing and *before* committing to a specific publishing track because the consequences of publishing choices can determine whether an author gets her book in a store and/or has bookstore events at all.

For some writers, getting the book into print *is* the goal; they may not care about doing events. If your goals include author events, having a clear sense of how you and your material may best translate into a live event is important, as is being open to suggestions and opportunities that may differ from that vision. For various reasons, not all bookstores will be able to help bring your event vision into reality, but being clear and open is a great start.

As an event coordinator, I would often receive event requests from underprepared writers who had published a book and wanted an event, but they seemed to think that because they had a book, they were done. The problem was, these writers didn't realize what they needed to know about publishing, distribution, bookstores, and author events. Finishing their books was just a beginning, and they actually may have made some decisions en route to publication that could work *against* them in realizing their goals of getting their books in bookstores and securing author events for themselves.

What should authors consider before approaching a bookstore about the possibility of an author event?
They should be aware that net profit margins for bookstores are *very, very* low, and brick-and-mortar bookstores are ever more challenged to stay in business. In order to host an author event, a bookstore needs to be able to get a given title into the store on terms that work for its store for events (see below for details on this).

It costs resources of time and of money to stock and sell books, as well as to put on author events. Some stores ask authors and/or publishers to share directly and financially in this cost. Some publishers support authors by providing travel expenses, publicity materials, review copies, and something called "co-op," which is financial support to bookstores for promotions that may or may not be tied to events. An individual book is part of a much bigger, ever-shifting puzzle that each bookstore has to manage; different stores manage this differently.

Authors should also know that having an event can become part of a relationship. Brick-and-mortar bookstores, especially independent ones, are often community hubs, and thus more than "just bookstores." Because of this, relationships matter.

What are the "terms," mentioned above, that authors need to be aware of?

From a bookstore perspective, "terms" are the conditions under which books are available to a given store. Terms are relevant to *standard ordering* (books ordered from publishers or a third-party wholesaler or distributor; availability of a title doesn't necessarily equal acceptable terms for a store), *event ordering* (orders for multiple copies of a title in support of an event, usually ordered several weeks early for pre-event displays and sales), and *consignment* (a direct agreement between the bookstore and either a publisher or the author, used when standard ordering isn't a viable option; the bookstore generally sets the terms, which may include a consignment fee and/or shipping costs).

Terms can be a "make or break" reason why a bookstore does or does not order a book into its inventory. It's important to note that the specifics of terms for standard ordering versus event ordering may vary, and a key factor in determining whether a bookstore will agree to host an author event is whether a given title is available to the bookstore on terms that work *for its events program.*

Specific terms available to bookstores may vary from bookstore to bookstore, but the categories of terms that bookstores consider are universal:

- Discounts: What does the store have to pay for each copy of the book? The standard minimum discount is 40-45% off cover/retail price.

- Freight: Will the publisher/distributor/wholesaler pay the book freight? Both ways? And if free freight is available, is there a minimum required order to receive it?

- Returns/penalties: Does the store have to pay a penalty and/or return freight to return unsold copies?

- Payment: When does the bookstore have to pay for the books?

What are some of the factors that a bookstore event coordinator may consider when deciding whether to host an event for a particular author/book?

Similar to questions a general bookstore buyer may ask when deciding whether to add a book to inventory, here are a few questions event coordinators may ask themselves:

- Will the book (topic, genre, writing style, local relevance, etc.) appeal to our customers and likely result in sales?

- Is the book available to us on terms that work for us for events?

- When was it or will it be published? If it's already published, is it older than six months, a year?

- If the author has previously published, have we sold her/his books, and if so, how were sales?

- Do we have a relationship with the author, and/or

does the author have local connections?

- Do we have an established relationship with the source of the book? If not, what terms are available, and is establishing a relationship likely to be a wise use of time and resources?

- Is there buzz about this book among independent bookstores, within the larger industry, and/or in the media generally?

- Is someone on our staff fired up about this book/author?

- Is the book a likely candidate for hand-selling?

- In what formats is it/will it be available?

- Does the author support independent bookstores (e.g., through relationships, website, blog posts)?

- If the author has a website, does he or she link to independent bookstores or IndieBound? Amazon? Barnes & Noble?

- What outreach is the publisher/author doing to support sales and visibility of the book?

- When is payment due?

Key considerations for event coordinators are whether they believe the book will be of interest to the store's customers and result in event turnout; whether the purchasing terms are acceptable for events; whether the book is forthcoming, or published six or fewer months earlier; whether free freight and penalty-free returns are available; and when payment is due.

What should authors know about bookstore events before requesting an event?

When I was at Village Books, we hosted author events that had various components. Most included Q&As and signings at the end, and many included readings from the book. Rarely did we host just a signing where an author sits and signs books, though some stores do. With each event coordinator, consider asking whether there is a presentation format that works best with the store's audience, and be clear about what you can offer.

I believe it's also important for authors, especially those who wish to have bookstore events, to support real, brick-and-mortar bookstores and to build professional relationships with store staff. It's not just good for individual authors; it's good for the industry, the bookstores, and the communities in which bookstores exist. Events can obviously happen at venues other than bookstores, but even for non-bookstore events, a bookstore is often involved in providing books.

Event coordinators at bookstores with strong event programs receive and send literally hundreds of e-mails each week. As an author requesting an event, you want to stand out, but only in a good way. Professionalism and patience are good qualities to nurture when requesting an event. In contacting a venue, *request* an event and thank the event coordinator for considering your request. Though it may be a strong desire, having an event at a given venue is not a given. If the answer is no, try to leave the door open by how you respond; handled well, it could lead to a future event and/or building that professional relationship.

Different bookstores do things differently, both in terms of ordering/stocking books and in setting up and promoting events. Stores may have a single event coordinator or may split event coordination among two or more staff members. Many event programs, especially those that are robust, often schedule out three months or more; for touring authors published and supported by major presses, sometimes events are scheduled six months out. Though multiple factors contribute to this timing, key among them is promotional lead time.

What is the best way for a local author to approach a bookstore to request an event, and what details should the author be prepared to provide to booksellers?
I believe the best way for an author to approach a bookstore for the possibility of an event is with grace and gratitude. At its best, the relationship between an author and a bookstore is symbiotic, wherein both have much to offer. Whatever a bookstore is willing to do on behalf of an author is a gift. In turn, the author and his/her book may bring customers into the store, engage them in conversation, and ultimately result in sales.

Being fully prepared can help maximize the potential of having an event at a desired venue, local or not. To discern whether your local store might be a good match for an event, consider some key information about the bookstore *before* getting in touch. Does it offer an events program or just do occasional events, and how many? What kinds of events does the store host? If you haven't already, attend and "study" several events at the store to get a sense of the events program, typical formats, and how other authors present in that setting.

Try to find out how each bookstore event coordinator likes to be contacted and what information each wants on first contact, and then do it that way. What bookstores will ask for varies, but presenting this information succinctly shows professionalism and makes it easier for an event coordinator to make an informed decision about whether to offer an event.

Some basics to have ready to send via e-mail before making contact are:

- Book title
- Author name(s)
- 13-digit ISBN
- Format(s): paper/hardback, e-book, audio book, etc.
- Publisher
- Publication date
- Genre(s), i.e., where it would be shelved in the store
- How it's available to bookstores (*not* Amazon or other online retailers)
- Book synopsis (twenty-five to fifty words)
- Author bio (twenty-five to fifty words)
- An author website link is helpful, but an e-mail with the above info all in one place is best. If you have a website, include your link in addition to—not in place of—the information above.

Have ready, but do not send unless requested, high-resolution JPEGs of an author photo and front book cover. Having reviews, blurbs, specific event ideas, and information on promotions and how/whether you use social media may be helpful as well. Note that you may be asked about your previous event and/or public speaking experience.

A few things to avoid when requesting an event include:

- Inquiring about the possibility of an event without sufficient lead time.

- Sending a mass, impersonal e-mail to several bookstores asking for events.

- Sending an e-mail with huge attachments (e.g., head shots or book jackets) that clog up an event coordinator's e-mail inbox.

- Lacking patience in the communication process with event coordinators.

- Approaching an event coordinator with arrogance or a sense of entitlement.

- Not knowing the difference between retail and wholesale availability, and demonstrating this by telling an indie bookstore employee—when asked how the book is available to bookstores—that the book is "available on Amazon."

What should an author do to help promote a bookstore event?

Bookstores vary in how much and what kind of outreach they do for their events, as well as in the promotional deadlines and requirements they may have for promoting an event; what's standard at one store may be rare at another. In securing an event with a particular bookstore, find out about the store's event marketing and promotional efforts and time lines, and about what expectations and requests the event coordinator may have. Be able to articulate how you can promote the event in the effort to get people to turn out.

Will you have posters or postcards? If so, can you customize them with event info, the venue name, and the address? Find out if the store has preferences related to this, and try to meet them if possible.

Do you have a mailing list or other contacts in the desired

event area? Are you affiliated with a group or organization that might be willing to help promote (e.g., through a newsletter) and maybe co-present the event? Do you have a blog, website, Facebook page, or Twitter following? Can you arrange or are you already scheduled for a TV or radio interview that might allow you to promote your event?

A few examples of efforts a bookstore might undertake to promote an event include sending press releases to local newspapers, magazines, and radio and TV stations; entering event information into the bookstore web event calendar and community event calendars; creating in-store promotions such as dedicated event displays, shelf-tags, posters, and reader boards; placing author- or publisher-provided bookmarks or postcards in inventoried books and/or on counters; using e-mail promotions and social media; and doing specific outreach to groups or organizations that may be interested in a book's content or author.

For a bookstore, what makes a successful author event?
From my perspective, author events are about getting people into the store, creating an experience around a book and its author, engaging and bolstering community, exchanging ideas, and yes, selling books. It's important to note that "successful" doesn't necessarily equate to large or elaborate but rather has more to do with the energy of the event and whether the author and audience connect.

While authors, publicists, and event coordinators alike might strive for and love capacity crowds, from my perspective it's not completely about the number of people who show up. It's also about how those who do show up engage with the author, and vice versa. Authors, especially newer authors, who rate the success of their events by the number of people who show up may set themselves up for disappointment. If possible, try to arrange to have familiar faces in the audience. It may mean speaking to mostly familiars, but at least there's an audience. If no one shows up—believe it or not, it can happen—then use it as an opportunity to talk with staff if they are available and to build your relationship with that store. Some of the best events I've attended have been on the small side, which has allowed the audience to engage with the author fully.

Book sales matter, especially these days. There is a concept called "sell-through rate," which can help put event sales in perspective. This number is arrived at by dividing the number of books sold at the event by the number of people attending the event. Let's say a store sells ten books at an event that fifty people attend. That's a sell-through rate of 20 percent. And that's a respectable number.

Matching an event to your book, your style, and a venue's possibilities is key. If bringing an idea to life will cost extra time (e.g., to decorate a venue) or money (e.g., for art supplies, treats, or tchotchkes), be prepared to offer human power, supplies, and/or funds to make it happen. Authors have had their events, especially book launches, catered with special themed cakes and party favors for the audience. Sometimes related craft projects, games, food tastings, or skill demonstrations were part of an event. Sometimes there were publisher or sponsor giveaways. Once we even turned the event space into a jazz club for the backdrop of an event. The possibilities are endless.

Inspiration

AUTHOR JENNA BLUM

Jenna Blum is the *New York Times* and international bestselling author of *Those Who Save Us* and *The Stormchasers* and is one of Oprah's Top Thirty Women Writers. Her debut novel, *Those Who Save Us*—a *New York Times* bestseller, #1 Book of 2011 in Holland, and *Boston Globe* bestseller—received the 2005 Ribalow Prize, judged by Elie Wiesel. *The Stormchasers* is also a Dutch bestseller, a *Boston Globe* bestseller, and a Target Emerging Author Pick. Jenna lives with photographer Jim Reed and black Lab Woodrow in Wichita, Kansas, where she is writing the screenplay for *Those Who Save Us*.

Tell us about the journey of *Those Who Save Us* from debut novel to international bestseller: How long did it take?

Those Who Save Us came out in 2004 in hardcover—a.k.a. the family and friends edition, because that's who bought it. It was published in 2005 in paperback, and I knew that was its second and last lease on life. I figured at that point I'd throw everything I had at the wall and see what stuck, promotionally. What did I have to lose? I loved my book. I spent years of my life researching and writing it because I loved it, and if I could do anything I could to keep it from falling down the well without a sound, I'd do it.

I had incredible help from readers, and the way this happened was, I started going to book clubs. The mother of one of my novelists at Grub Street Writers in Boston invited me to her book club, and of course I went. A chance to talk about my baby for three hours with kind strangers and drink all their wine? What writer wouldn't go? Mrs. Garabedian, my first book club hostess, was so kind to me. She and her group gave me an orchid, which I still have and which still blooms. They recommended me to another book club—which cooked German food featured in the book, I might add. And that book club recommended me to another. By the time *Those Who Save Us* jumped onto the *New York Times* bestseller list in 2008, three years after it had come out in paperback, I was speaking at three book clubs a day (!) in person, and talking to as many as I could by phone. I estimate I visited over 1,000 book clubs in the Boston area alone, and it was a great privilege. Now readers in Holland and European countries are kindly keeping the book aloft. *Those Who Save Us* is a reader-created book, which I think is just as it should be.

Did you always believe it would be as hugely successful as it was?

I hoped it would be. I suppose many writers are prone to delusions of grandeur, fantasies we use to sustain ourselves through the ritual and daily humiliations of writer's block, rejections, and bad reviews. I'm no exception. When I was writing *Those Who Save Us*, I used to walk down by the Charles River in Boston and imagine myself talking to Katie Couric on the *Today Show* ... to Oprah ... which actor would play what character in the movie version ... what I would wear to the Oscars ... Yet when *Those Who Save Us* did make the *NYT* list, it was a miracle I've never stopped being grateful for. Once, en route to a book club in Long Island, I drove past the *NYT* headquarters and yelled, "Thank you for my life!" I thank Providence and readers every single day for what has happened to this book.

What were some of the major factors of its success?
I suppose this is redundant by now, but—readers! Also, Borders chose *Those Who Save Us* for their Book Club pick, and for a two-for-one promotion, for almost two years. Such is the power of bookstores, which is why I so deeply and heartily lament the loss of them. Every bookstore that closes is a light going out. Please, buy real books!

What do you think are the most important things for a new author to keep in mind when it comes to reaching his/her readers?
Not to be discouraged. My agent always says, "A book is sold one book at a time," and that's true. Whatever you can do to sell one book, do it! That's one more person reading your beloved baby.

Also, try everything that feels organic to you. If you hate social media, don't do social media. But make lists of things you *do* like to do, and do them on behalf of your book. Think outside the covers. If you like to bake, send cookies with your book's cover on it to booksellers. If you sing, go busk with your book in the subway. If you're shy, put business cards with your book's cover on them beneath windshield wipers, on Starbucks bulletin boards. Why not? What do you have to lose?

Finally, you can never be too humble. I've done readings with audiences of five hundred. I've done readings with audiences of two—my mom and a homeless guy. If I sell one book, if the homeless guy liked what I read, well, that's why I write.

What advice do you have for authors who find themselves worn down by the often daunting and seemingly never-ending process of book promotion?
You don't have to do everything. Publicists will tell you that you *have* to have a blog. I have a blog. I rarely add to it. But I do a lot of book clubs via Skype and phone, and I'm a Facebook/Twitter addict. Find what you love (or can stand), and do it regularly. Ration it out in digestible time bites and, for the love of God, put it on your to-do list/calendar, on "repeat weekly," with reminders. Marketing your book is as valid a form of work as any other.

Never give in, never give in, never give in!

$\backsim$

About the author

Midge Raymond has been a writer, editor, and teacher for more than twenty years. She has taught at Boston University, Grub Street, San Diego Writers, and Richard Hugo House, among others.

Midge's short story collection, *Forgetting English*, received the Spokane Prize for Short Fiction. Originally published by Eastern Washington University Press, the book was reissued in an expanded edition by Press 53 in 2011. Her award-winning stories have appeared in numerous literary journals and magazines, including *TriQuarterly, American Literary Review, Bellingham Review, Indiana Review, North American Review, Bellevue Literary Review,* and the *Los Angeles Times.* For more information, visit www.MidgeRaymond.com.

Everyday Writing: Tips and prompts to fit your regularly scheduled life

"Raymond has a gift for dispensing gentle, intelligent advice that even the most harried and overworked will find inspiring."
— *The Writer* magazine

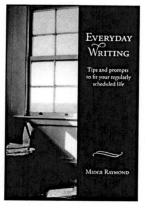

Writers are often told that in order to succeed, they must write every day—yet this isn't realistic or feasible for writers with families, day jobs, and other responsibilities that preclude a daily writing practice.

Everyday Writing is about how to be a writer every day, even if you're unable to sit down to write every day.

This book provides dozens of tips for busy writers, including how to create your ideal writing space, how to develop habits that work for you, and how to keep your projects moving forward even when you're short on time. *Everyday Writing* also offers more than 150 prompts to fit into any writer's life, from five-minute prompts you can do in a grocery store line to lengthy prompts that are perfect for a writing retreat. Whether you'd like to generate new material, free yourself from writer's block, or start a revision, these writing exercises provide a way to engage immediately with your work.

"Practical and encouraging with refreshing touches of humor...If you're a writer looking for a friendly companion and supportive coach for your writing life, you'll find her living in the pages of *Everyday Writing*."
—Judy Reeves, author of *A Writer's Book of Days*

Ashland Creek Press is a small, independent publisher of books with a world view. From travel narratives to eco-literature, our mission is to publish a range of books that foster an appreciation for worlds outside our own, for nature and the animal kingdom, for the creative process, and for the ways in which we all connect. To keep up-to-date on new and forthcoming works, subscribe to our free newsletter by visiting www.AshlandCreekPress.com.

CPSIA information can be obtained at www.ICGtesting.com
Printed in the USA
BVOW07s1956250914

367966BV00001B/1/P